OXFORD TYPE

An Anthology of *Isis*, the Oxford
University Magazine

Edited and with an introduction by
Andrew Billen and *Mark Skipworth*

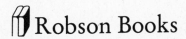 Robson Books

FIRST PUBLISHED IN GREAT BRITAIN IN 1984
BY ROBSON BOOKS LTD., BOLSOVER HOUSE,
5-6 CLIPSTONE STREET, LONDON W1P 7CB.
COPYRIGHT © 1984 *ISIS* AND CONTRIBUTORS.
INTRODUCTION COPYRIGHT © 1984 ANDREW
BILLEN AND MARK SKIPWORTH

British Library Cataloguing in Publication Data

Oxford Type

1.   Anthologies
1.   Billen, Andrew   2.   Skipworth, Mark
082   PN6014

ISBN 0-86051-213-4

Printed in Great Britain by Redwood Burn Ltd., Trowbridge

CONTENTS

1945 - 1959

The Sixties and After

Acknowledgements

We are grateful to the board of Isis Publications Ltd for their permission and enthusiasm for this book; Mr Peter Burrows of Holywell Press for his help with the history of *Isis* and the loan of a number of photographs; the Oxford Union and its library staff for filling in the gaps where the magazine's own records proved deficient; Miss Stephanie Billen, Mr Paul Giles, Mr David Thomas and Mr Gary Bricklebank for putting us up on numerous trips to Oxford and London; Mrs Julie Skipworth for helping in the research and her patience during long evenings in which she was deprived of a husband.

We would also like to thank Mr David Flynn, the then editor of the Sheffield *Star*, who gave us permission to take on this outside work.

Our principal debt is, however, to the contributors for their good wishes, despite their concern about what might be exhumed from their student days. The piece of Max Beerbohm appears by permission of his sister-in-law Eva Reichmann, and Ken Tynan's review by that of the Tynan Estate; it was reprinted by Longman in *He That Plays The King*. The poem 'Vicarious Vengeance' appears by permission of the estate of the late Sir Alan Herbert.

We hope proceeds from this book help *Isis* overcome its present financial difficulties.

Sheffield, 1984   A.B.
                                                          M.S.

Introduction

> *'When the High Lama asked him whether Shangri-la*
> *was not unique in his experience, and if the Western*
> *world could offer anything in the least like it, he*
> *answered with a smile: 'Well, yes–to be quite frank, it*
> *reminds me very slightly of Oxford.'*–James Hilton,
> Lost Horizon

Isis—or rather *The Isis*, for it took the radicalism of the late
1950s to discard the definite article—was born in Oxford on
April 27, 1892, founded by Mostyn Turtle Piggott, the first of
a long line of student editors whose only shared trait was an
ambition to write.

The magazine's name is taken from that stretch of the
Thames which flows through the oldest of Britain's university
cities. For more than half a century, *Isis* was bonded to the
local printers and publishers, Holywell Press, whose proprietor
Harry Burrows realised that narcissistic Oxford would enjoy
gazing at itself in a weekly looking-glass. The deal was simple.
He would allow students to decide content so long as they paid
deference to the standards he set for profit and taste. An
unruly generation of later times would discover to their cost
the extent of Mr Burrows' bailiwick.

The university had rarely brooked the intrusion of the wider
world into its domain, preferring to construct its own

Lilliputian skyscape of institutions. That the Oxford Union Society was, for example, less in earnest than Parliament merely confirmed its superiority over the establishment it apparently aped. As painstaking recorder of university minutiae, *The Isis* was all the more welcome for the tongue in its cheek. Within its eight pages, assiduous reports of Oxford Union debates, rugby matches and university theatre were laced with ribbing asides and jocular verse. The first editorial, 'Our Programme', affirmed:

> 'We have no politics and fewer principles, and should we last until the General Election we shall use our influence for neither side. We shall endeavour to be humorous without being ill-humoured, critical without being captious, militant without being malevolent, independent without being impertinent, and funny (as Mr Albert Chevalier says) without being vulgar.'

These were words that years later Holywell would use to call to heel a rebellious staff intent on taking sides and courting the tag of impertinence.

In 1893, *The Isis* was forced to double its price to the then not inconsiderable sum of sixpence. But perhaps the blow to readers was softened by the first appearance of the magazine's most famous feature, the *Isis* 'Idol'. The 'Idol' was a portrait of a leading personality at the university—in the early days most often a sportsman. Lest these subjects should find the glare of publicity too invidious, they were invited to nominate a friend to write the piece. Thus, whatever the original intention, 'idol' was no ironic sobriquet, although in many cases writers would resort—uneasily—to flippancy as a guard against the excesses of unrestrained worship.

Presidency of OUDS, the university drama society, or the Union, would ensure the 'Idol' treatment. Even then, the president's athletic prowess was loudly advertised. The only other sure way of winning the accolade was to edit *The Isis*, and after the second world war it became customary to carry an Idol on the outgoing editor in the first of the following term's magazines. This, of course, neatly ensured survival of what was by then an outmoded series. For which editor would destroy a pedestal upon which he could look forward soon to be so decorously placed? The necessary courage was found finally by Dennis Potter in 1958. The 'Idol' has been subsequently resurrected, but briefly and in different forms: in the Sixties a transcript interview replaced the hagiography; a year or so ago the idea was turned on its head so that a satirical sketch appeared, written by anyone but the victim's friend.

The first 'Idol' was Mr Cecil Douglas Baker, captain of the rugby XV and the possessor of a 'fine bass voice of more than ordinary compass'. Other pre-1939 'Idols' (when the tone was surest) were Neville Coghill, Lord David Cecil, Quentin Hogg (Union president in 1929), the entire 1932 boat race team, C. B. Fry (a record three times) and T. E. Lawrence (Arabia, Jesus and All Souls). The 'Idol's' popularity was such that they were reprinted separately and sold for a penny a piece, though the first woman 'Idol' (Lady Katherine Cairns) had to wait until 1935.

Read today they are hardly ever less than slightly absurd. The recipe was to begin with a joke or two about remarkable stellar occurrences at the subject's birth, add an innocuous anecdote illustrating his precocity at school, and then seal with sweet reports of his instant popularity at Oxford. Sometimes the conclusion was disastrously bathetic. Of a certain rugby star, the 'Idol' said:

> 'That he has not entered the Diplomatic Service must be a source of regret to all those who have their country's welfare at heart. Instead he has devoted his energies to freemasonry and hunting.'

In a 1938 apologia, the role of 'sycophant to perfection' was defended on the grounds that it was bestowed only on those Oxford successes already 'glutted with praise and congratulation'. Michael Arnott, writing in the Fifties, pointed out that many tributes went to people whose tragic deaths in the war entombed their early promise. He added the 'Idol' was 'less an introduction than a coronation, a strange sort of coronation, that is held at the end of a reign, a coronation that is also a Viking funeral, to send its subject out into the world beyond wreathed in a cloud of glory.'

13

Yet, for all the indulgent prose, *The Isis* of before the Great War could boast remarkable recruits—Max Beerbohm, Hilaire Belloc, John Buchan, A. P. Herbert and Compton Mackenzie. Shutting his ears for a moment to Eights Week's laughing flow of cocktails, one leader writer in the summer of 1914 sensed what was to come:

> '. . . in Metternichean phraseology, the conflagration must be allowed to burn itself out. But there will be precious little left at the end to our way of thinking.'

For more than four years *The Isis* ceased publication. A later writer estimated that of hundreds of 'Idols' in the decade before the war, two-thirds were killed.

On a spring day in 1919, a young man walked into Holywell Press, announced that he wished to start up *The Isis* again and asked if they would wish to print it. Replying that being the owners they would be much put out if anyone else did, Holywell appointed him editor. So Beverley Nichols launched the post-war *Isis*, proving one of its most brilliant editors. It was as if he half-believed that merely by writing about the Oxford he had dreamed of, he could create it. Afterwards he was to say with modesty, without *The Isis* 'a note in the Oxford orchestra was missing'.

But until the first issue there was scant enthusiasm for his vision. Without staff, Nichols was forced to produce the opening number himself, assuming the distinctive voices of the leader writer, the gossip columnist of 'Heard in the High' and the sports reporter. He even involved himself in the lay-out. Hindered by the paper shortage, the magazine was less glossy and for a time emerged only fortnightly. Undaunted, Nichols assuredly re-established its aims:

> '. . . the great fact remains [he wrote in the first leader] that Oxford is still here, a little dazed and unsteady perhaps, but Oxford all the same, and it is to sing of Oxford that *The Isis* appears once more, to reflect its every tendency, to echo its laughter and—well, to do the other thing.'

Soon he was scolding his readers.

'We never get anything but verse; we seldom get any poetry. Why is it that people are incapable of writing anything except in metre? Why must they burst into song when talking about the Broad, and try their hand at triolets when they talk about the Turl? Why can they not write to us in a letter beginning "Dear Sir" and ending "Yours sincerely", instead of beginning "Heavenly Muse", and ending with "The scarlet panoplies of Hell"? We are disappointed in you, fond reader. You haven't got over the war yet and we feel, especially just before going to print, that the iron indeed has entered your soul.'

In his Oxford bags Nichols swaggered out of the khaki shadow. With demonic energy he founded a new literary magazine, revived the Liberal Club, made his debut as a concert pianist and became President of the Union . . . all of it in the eighteen months before his father, in an alcoholic spasm, withdrew financial support and he had to leave.

Whirling into the socialite Twenties, *The Isis*, which by now had incorporated the rival *Varsity* magazine, became the party-goer's journal, the aesthete's 'rag'. It was *The Isis* that the aesthete Sebastian Flyte dismissed scornfully in Evelyn Waugh's *Brideshead Revisited*. Even Harold Acton, remembered by his close friend Waugh for reading *The Waste Land* through a megaphone, was made to toe the party line. 'His contempt for aesthetes is unbounded,' a 1924 Idol insisted. Only the social colossus Waugh managed to bestride both camps. He simultaneously wrote Union notes for *The Isis* and its most enduring competitor, the recently re-born *Cherwell*. At that time, *Cherwell* aligned itself with the aesthete faction while *The Isis* remained steadfast in its loyalty to Oxford's own version of the Three Rs—rowing, rugger and revelry. Today, the roles have been reversed.

Unerringly, the Twenties' *Isis* rooted for the Establishment on a gamut of political controversies, offending the finer sensibilities of later contributors. In 1920, during a local bus strike, it condemned out of hand members of Ruskin Hall, the trade union college, and the Labour Club for 'advocating revolutionary doctrines calculated to influence the mob to acts of violence.' Six years later, as the country lurched into a general strike, it concocted an easy solution to the miners' anger at a cut in pay:

> 'If free beer were supplied to the miners on entering and leaving the mines, they would never want to strike.'

By the next issue the staff had left Oxford to do their bit to keep the country running during the strike. Amid much coy speculation on what effect all the exercise would have on the sportsmen, the men spiritedly heaved sacks and drove fruit trucks in Covent Garden. *The Isis* of May 12 declared:

> 'In the absence of the entire male editorial staff on National Service, the Lady Editor has stepped courage-ously into the breach, and unless the entire varsity goes down, *The Isis* will be carried on by the undergraduates for the remainder of the strike.'

In allowing women to take the reins for a few issues, *The Isis* deserves perhaps a small footnote in the history of women at the university. In 1924 Dilys Powell began a bluntly feminist series of articles called 'What Every Woman Thinks'. Although she posted her copy and never met the other members of staff, they did back her polemics on the anchorite restrictions imposed on undergraduettes. These were chiefly the univer-sity's insistence on chaperones for women whenever they ventured beyond their single-sex colleges and strict rules on when they should be back. On the latter, the issue of June 4, 1924 carried a plea that women 'might occasionally be allowed to see the end of a play in Oxford'. On the former, Dilys Powell opined that the chaperones must in reality be for the protection of the men. An anonymous woman correspondent, complaining of being escorted to her tutor's lodgings, exclaimed:

> 'I am gratified to feel that I am worth so much attention and care, but at the same time I am horrified at the wickedness of these naughty old dons, on whose account such precautions are necessary.
> 'Will you exert your influence either to have the

university regulations revised, or else to have the most dangerous of these old reprobates removed?'

But while calling for the rescinding of the rules, *The Isis* couched the appeal in distinctly unfeminist terms:

'A certain undergraduate I am informed was observed on the last day of eights in a punt with one man at four o'clock; taking tea with another on a college barge at five; and driving out to dinner with her third victim at six-thirty. If I were a cynic (but I am too young) I should suggest that any girl who can give three men such a valuable object lesson in the fickleness of her sex in the short space of three hours, is an educational institution of first-rate importance, and should be recognised as such by the state.'

A fierce attack on the state of women's colleges by Dilys Powell provoked a demand for retribution from their heads. The Vice-Chancellor was prevailed upon to send down *The Isis*'s deputy editor, Gerald Gardiner, then also president of the Union and later Lord Chancellor in the Wilson government. The severity of the punishment was mitigated by the fact that he had already taken his degree.

By this time *The Isis* had moved with Holywell Press to premises at the back of Christ Church in Alfred Street. But you were just as likely to find the editor and staff in The Bear, a pub only yards away. A long-suffering printer recalled that one editor of the early Twenties appeared to live there solely on whisky and dry biscuits. Another, 'the laziest of the lot', used to have the proofs sent round to him in bed. Frequently, the printers took editorial decisions by default, hacking pieces until they fitted in order to meet the publication deadline. Idleness may have infuriated the printers but mere diligence was not always enough. The owners saw fit to sack from the editorship a young man who worked 'like a Trojan, but was not considered good enough for the job'. Retaliating, the outcast was responsible for reviving *Cherwell*.

The Isis of the Thirties averted its gaze from the political eruptions in Europe, but then, so did *The Times*. One editorial mooted that the thing to remember about Germany's new chancellor was that he looked so funny on newsreels. In 1933, the magazine supported the Union's notorious passing of the motion 'That this house would in no circumstances fight for its king and country'. As Fleet Street descended on Oxford to find out what had happened to the finest of the nation's youth, the leader writer trumpeted: 'If anyone calls us cowards we will gladly black his eye.' Two years later the paper lowered its price to threepence and repudiated 'intellectual snobbery and prolonged feuds with university politicians'. Soon it was selling 1,250 copies a week. In October, 1935, Hitler banned it from Germany—*The Isis* gloated but was puzzled about what it had done to merit his attention. In future, it decided, its German subscribers would receive their copies bound in the covers of film magazines.

Despite Airey Neave's anti-fascist short stories, for the most part the magazine had its head firmly in the sand. Interviews started up with showbiz figures like band leader Billy Cotton and film star Robert Donat. Eight pages were now devoted to sport. In June, 1939, the Union notes recorded an ill-attended debate on the motion 'This house urges the Polish Government to resist any attempts to incorporate Danzig within the German Reich' (carried 51 votes to 19). But the editorial writers were more anxious about tourists in Oxford than armies in Europe. Ironically, only the 'George Baxter' sports diarist hinted that an era was ending, in the final pre-war issue:

'The world is in a permanent state of flux, and with such an apothegm Baxter bids his readers a final farewell.'

For the duration of the war, no *Isis* appeared. Echoing an earlier lament, its 1936 editor Keith Bryant mourned afterwards that more than half his staff had not survived the war. But *The Isis* survived, emerging fighting fit on November 28, 1945. With no rivals on sale yet, the first issue sold out and Holywell made room for a staff office on the ground floor of their works.

The late Forties forged a new resilience in the magazine, straightforward ex-soldiers tempering the optimism of younger men too young to fight but impatient to rebuild. Here was a new generation of talent—Kenneth Tynan, Lindsay Anderson, Kenneth Harris, Ludovic Kennedy, Peter Parker, Alan Brien. For the first time, journalism became a proper subject for serious discussion. Ludovic Kennedy prodded the soft underbelly of sluggish news stories in an article 'Let us Debunk Famous Men'. Believing it to be dishonest, Derek Cooper stripped bare the plebeian veneer of the Old Codgers letter column in the *Daily Mirror*. A good-humoured reply came back from the varnisher—the Old Codger revealed as a with-it Oxford graduate. For the arts, Tynan wrote what some believe to have been his most exuberant theatre criticism, whilst Anderson cut his teeth on the celluloid images that flickered across the screens of Oxford's Scala and Electra. (He liked *Pinnochio*.)

Not even the 1947 fuel crisis could douse the magazine's energy. Emmanuel Shinwell, the minister responsible for the conservation of power, banned the use of electricity for publishing periodicals. Undeterred, the *Isis* mavericks compiled a four-page broadsheet, set by hand and printed by operating the treadle of a small press, everyone lending a foot in turn. When 300 had been printed and were ready for binding, the man from the ministry rang up to forbid distribution. The editor, Gwyl Owen, responded by going across to the Bear for a quick one. By the time he returned the copies had been stolen and mysteriously appeared on sale in colleges the next day. The broadsheet boasted 'most of the staple diet is here but condensed to vitamin tablets', and impishly introduced itself as:

'. . . wholly and solely a gesture in these starving days, an aperitif from the locked cellar; a late valentine from this welter of new-fledged Caxtons to the streets where men grow loud on the survival of the press and silent flow the dons.'

There were questions in Parliament.

The liveliness ran into and through the Fifties, but the voice grew harsher and the content switched from an infatuation with the arts to an obsession with politics. Some of the angriest young men, *pace* Amis and Osborne, could be found

19

spending their fury in *Isis* between 1957 and 1960. When the Bomb issue was dropped on the rest of the country in February, 1958, the commotion woke everyone. What raised hackles in high places was not the anti-nuclear posturing, but a half-page article titled 'Frontier Incidents—Exposure'. Keener to take the platform to lambast the general rather than the particular iniquities of defence policy, the editors relegated the piece to the bottom of page 12. Written by two ex-national service undergraduates, William Miller and Paul Thompson, it described how British Intelligence units provoked Russian troops into exposing their formations. The authors explained the incident had failed to come to light until now because of the Official Secrets Act. They were right; after various national papers swooped on the revelations, the pair were prosecuted under the Act. *Isis* hardly knew what had hit it. Returning after the spring vacation, the new editor, Dennis Potter, struck out wildly at the press:

> 'At this stage it would be injudicious and perhaps dangerous to make any comment whatever on the rights and wrongs of that unhappy *Isis* article in the H-bomb issue. That issue of course was compiled by dupes or agents of "one of the biggest spy rings in Europe", unearthed by a peculiarly active *Daily Sketch* reporter.'

He went on:

> 'But something needs to be said about the shabby little band of so-called journalists which descended upon Oxford at the end of last term . . . Cheating and lying aside, reporters made life intolerable for some people for a few days.'

The next issue carried an apology to one reporter accused of lying—Nicholas Tomalin, then of the *Daily Express*. And wisely, *Isis* set up a defence fund for Miller and Thompson, which eventually raised £541. A May issue recorded letters of support from J. B. Priestley, Tynan, Anderson and the novelist Doris Lessing. It agreed with the *New Statesman*'s observations that the offending article had been unlikely to tell a foreign power anything it did not already know, but, then, the Act was habitually used to keep information from the British public. Potter wrote:

> 'And so say all of us. On the other hand we have it on very good authority that a Mr Gavin Sorrell (is that how you spell it?), president or captain or whatever it is of the Oxford University Boat Club, thinks that Miller and Thompson ought to be strung up. We're so glad that we lost the boat race, and to observe that stupidity and incompetence are still closely linked.'

Another apology, for misquoting him, followed the week after. The agony was prolonged by fears that the appeal fund would not meet defence costs. The unfortunate writers in the end received prison sentences of three months and next term wrote thanking the well-wishers whose money 'gave us the legal help without which we might not have had the freedom to write this letter.'

The national controversy over the case and Potter's other broadsides on public figures, including royalty, claimed another casualty. If to Holywell the stylish Beverley Nichols had been the good Dr Jekyll, then miner's son Potter was a rabid Mr Hyde. In confusion, just before the last issue of the summer was due to be put together, Potter was ousted from the editor's chair. Whether he was sacked by the proprietors or he walked out under their pressure, was a matter of dispute. There is no doubt that the result was what, for all the flair of that term's *Isis*, Holywell had craved. Seizing the editorial column, the owners branded the past few issues 'as choice an exhibition of bad manners as has ever (dis)graced the pages of an intellectual magazine'. The crisis came about because Holywell defied convention by refusing Potter's nominee for next editor, Nicholas Deakin. Defending this, they wrote:

> 'Our action has not been an attempt to suppress or interfere with personal rights or liberties; nor has it been a breaking of a rule: it is the departure from a tradition which has been attended by obvious dangers. If the

21

objection is taken to this break in traditional practice, can the objection be fairly heard if in fact the general tone of *Isis* has been an attack on systems and institutions which are themselves largely traditional?'

They argued too that Potter had neglected properly to introduce them to his staff . . . an immensely able staff which included Perry Anderson, Kenith Trodd, Francis Hope and John Fuller. But their main objection was that the magazine was now 'definitely left-wing and will almost inevitably remain so'. The prospect was likely to damage sales and increase the risk of costly legal battles.

A letter published in the last issue of term from Stephen Hugh-Jones put the case for the defence:

'I do not question their legal right to do what they like with their own property; I recognise the business and legal risks they run, but I dispute, as I believe many people would, their moral right to treat a paper like a car, sprayed a different colour overnight.'

But Holywell's bid to appoint an outsider as editor failed when the entire student staff walked out in protest. Deakin became editor at the start of the new term after all.

Two years later there was a recrudescence in the diseased relations between the intimidated owners and the partisans it invited to produce its magazine. Editor Kenith Trodd had filled his spring term issues with writing much in the Potter mould. Speaking on behalf of other recent editors, he wrote expressing 'our distance from and embarrassment at Potter's excesses' but admitting 'our sympathy with nearly all his objectives'. Suddenly, Holywell decided enough really was enough. The outgoing editor's recommendation for successor was again rejected but this time new blood was successfully transfused. David Dimbleby, then a second-year Politics, Philosophy and Economics undergraduate at Christ Church, was appointed.

The next *Isis*, dated March 9, 1960—Trodd's last—exploded in anti-Dimbleby outrage. An open letter signed by Trodd and his staff read:

'The appointment of David Dimbleby to be the next editor of *Isis* is against the wishes and advice of the present editor and staff . . . we deplore the manner of the appointment. We also object to the principle that editorial policy should be subject to control by the proprietors, and will not therefore write or work under Dimbleby's editorship.'

Then Dennis Potter reappeared, like a banished son come to rub his hands at a family tragedy. By then at the BBC, he briefly turned his back on the cameras to recharge his old pen with vitriol:

'*Isis* is not just a gay and jolly newsheet for the benefit of friends, but also a magazine that has meant a great deal to many of us far too long for us not to feel sad and angry at this pitiful transformation.'

He added that he could not find it in his heart to blame Holywell:

'After all, when you have been trained to believe in the rigid application of tried and trusted values of unadulterated philistinism, bolstered up by what your small shopkeeper friends say about *Isis* and a respect for what Professor Roper [the chancellor] says about everything, then you would not take kindly to the striving incoherence and desperate earnestness of young men thirty years your junior.'

Another writer predicted 'an anodyne, non-political magazine, whose editor is reputed to be too nice to have any opinions at all and whose style, if family traditions are anything to go by, will combine the *Richmond and Twickenham Times* and the last coronation broadcast.'

Trodd, in 1980, spoke about what he called a *putsch*. 'Holywell felt we had got above our station,' he said, condemning Dimbleby partly because 'in terms of taste, I regarded his father as a walking embodiment of BBC Reithism. Dimbleby just wasn't my type.' Dimbleby, on the other hand, maintained

Isis had been 'frog-marched away from its old wide-ranging style reflecting Oxford life and made into a political magazine. People generally felt it was going down-hill, continually going on about workers at Cowley and run by a self-perpetuating minority almost exclusively Marxist.' He had approached Holywell with an idea for a magazine of his own and was invited instead to run *Isis*. The letter of protest from the staff claimed some bogus signatories and a few, like the late Francis Hope, kept writing.

At first Dimbleby found the going rough. 'Those who left sent me a copy of a new magazine they started up with a card saying "From some who have chosen to neither forgive nor forget". There was a lot of bitterness but I wasn't surprised; people don't give up power easily,' he recalled years after. He had also to meet the challenge from Holywell. For although he felt *Isis* had been hi-jacked from them, he did not wish to be under their thumb. A solution was finally found in the formation of a board to act as a buffer between editor and owner and to approve the appointment of successors. As it turned out, the doom merchants who forecast a return to flippancy were wrong, though the political hue softened. 'I suppose we became part of the centrist, liberal consensus,' Dimbleby offered. He resisted the temptation to dust down the Idol but did restore a full page of union notes. Ferdinand Mount wrote a weekly column that prefigured his mastery of the form in *The Spectator*. Peter Jay analysed in characteristically labyrinthine sentences the leadership of Mr Gaitskell, while his future wife, Margaret Callaghan, was features editor. Richard Ingrams was news editor and Auberon Waugh published his first work of fiction. Even Trodd used words no harsher than 'a brighter compromise' to describe the Dimbleby term.

But the Holywell days were nearly over. In the summer of 1963 the firm regretfully concluded they could no longer bear the responsibility or cost of running the magazine. Their greatest worry was the vast number of claims made against *Isis* by people who believed they had been defamed. Harry Burrows' grandson, Peter Burrows, told the present writers, 'We were being taken to the cleaners by everyone from pop stars to char ladies.' No doubt also, they felt the spirit of

Potter was still to be fully exorcised. When the paper was put up for sale, it must have seemed to many that the end was nigh.

Salvation came in the shape of socialist millionaire Robert Maxwell whose Pergamon Press publishing house was based in Oxford. Revealing his nascent designs on newspaper ownership, he bought *Isis* on condition it was turned into a national student paper. In a bizarre excursion, *Isis National* began distribution to other universities around the country early in 1964.

Editorially, however, *Isis* didn't know where it was going: one issue was devoted to analysis of the Joseph Losey film *The Servant*, whilst its parochialism was exposed in another by little notices like that advertising weekly news meetings, 'at 3pm in Balliol'. By February, the magazine claimed to be selling like hot cakes in Bangor and Aberystwyth, while Oxford's geographical and historical neighbours, Reading and Cambridge, were unimpressed. Few articles appeared from students of other universities, although one Edinburgh undergraduate wrote:

> 'I recently sent to you an article intended for *Isis National* entitled 'With Love/Hate from Me to You'. I am now convinced that this was a piece of ill-considered rubbish, a prime example of the provincial's Oxford complex. In the unlikely event of your having decided to publish it, I would be grateful if you would withdraw it, as publication would bring me into extreme disfavour up here. I enclose a 3d stamp for return.'

So the national experiment failed, but Maxwell remained a willing patron. *Isis* reproduced the heated rhetoric of youth rebellion in the Sixties without ever becoming a manifesto of revolution. An editor would proclaim his political commitment or Wilsonian interest in technology . . . one, it was said, conducted a 'grande affaire with steel and industrial pro-processes'—yet as often as not, his issues would be crammed with interviews with pop stars and chit-chat. A 1965 editor, Andrew Lawson, decided to 'Sod the general reader'. He proselytised that *Isis* should be:

'. . . a soap box on which committed people can stand up and YELL. Only when its articles are inspired by passion can this magazine *begin* to be of interest to its readers. To reverse this priority in an attempt to court the whole undergraduate population would involve us in a futile struggle with Oxford's extremes of cynicism and apathy.'

The next issue printed a letter appealing, 'Don't make me feel too uncomfortable, or passion could become a dirty word.' It was signed 'Sod, the general reader'. The lay-out of the magazine found its inspiration in the glossy Sunday magazines, and *Vogue* and *Viva*, rather than the thriving underground press. There was to be no orange text against a mauve wash in *Isis*.

In the summer of 1970 *Isis* came of age with the departure of its second owner, Maxwell. As a completely independent and student-owned publication, the magazine tried to broaden its base, this time scrapping the 'University' tag and asking to be accepted as Oxford Polytechnic's magazine too. Without a sugar-daddy to sweeten the monthly bank statements, editor Martin Meteyard took some unpalatable decisions. From its new offices in Frewin Court, *Isis* would now appear fortnightly with a hand-out called *Crisis* given away between issues. Answering a charge of hypocrisy in denouncing apartheid but using a full-page advertisement from Barclays Bank, which had interests in South Africa, Meteyard countered:

> 'There is no doubt in my mind that it is more useful to have a magazine with capitalist advertisements than no magazine at all.'

The formal link with the Polytechnic did not endure and *Crisis* died. *Isis* struggled on nevertheless, aided by the generosity of advertisers like Barclays.

For the student-run Isis Publications Ltd, as the new company was called, the Seventies and early Eighties were times of agonizing financial squeezes. The worst moment of all came early on. In January, 1972, the magazine confronted a print bill of a thousand pounds with a month in which to settle. So unlikely was it that such a sum could be raised in time that serious talks of a merger began with the equally impoverished arch-rival *Cherwell*. But help was at hand from an unexpected source. The cover of the January 28 issue was taken up by a telegram:

'READ OF YOUR FINANCIAL TROUBLES IN THE TIMES STOP ONE THOUSAND POUNDS WILL BE EN ROUTE AS SOON AS YOU CABLE US NAME AND ADDRESS OF PRINTERS AT THE GRANOTEL ROME—ELIZABETH TAYLOR AND RICHARD BURTON.'

Despite the windfall, the cruel paradox of autonomy was that, with all the battles against proprietors behind it, *Isis* had won only the freedom to go bust. In order to keep the magazine solvent, an editor could no longer afford to be merely an elegant stylist, he had to summon forth the patter of an advertising rep. In order to produce it, he needed the skilled eye of a newspaper page-planner—for the magazine was pasted together on the premises. Small wonder the only committed student writers the magazine attracted were those committed to the profession of journalism itself. Anthony Holden was perhaps the first of the breed, writing:

'. . . we're here to do more than tell you what a good time we all have producing this magazine. Nor are we here to declare war on our readers. We are here to perform no more than a service.'

Elsewhere, the studied cynicism of the decade prevailed. A 1973 'Private Isis' gossip columnist mocked:

'Sally Emerson, affectionately known as our editor, is anxious to meet a common, underprivileged girl for the magazine. If anyone feels herself to be a suitable case in point and would like to air her underprivileges, perhaps she would drop round for a chat, on, say, the problems of a proletarian in a middle-class university.'

The first editors were paid a generous £10 per term, but the real rewards were more intangible. Their power and social

27

standing in the undergraduate world were rivalled only by those of the Oxford Union president. Godfrey Smith, an *Isis* contributor and president of the Union, said there existed a crude balance of power between the two. He noted:

> 'Each is a species of producer, half artist, half administrator, wholly extrovert, who has eight performances for which he is absolutely responsible.'

The undertow of *Isis* tradition sometimes submerged the idiosyncrasies of an individual editor. Arthur Calder-Marshall observed how the personality of the magazine often triumphed. Remembering the condominium editorship of Anthony Gishford and Stefan Hopkinson in 1930, he wrote:

> 'Closing one's eyes in the later stages of dinner given by the editors, one found it impossible to tell whether it was Gishford or Hopkinson talking. Which, one wondered as the excellent port pursued its benevolent course, which is which? The answer, of course, was neither. Both were the editor of *The Isis*.'

Others, the most convinced of their talents, effortlessly moulded the magazine into their own image. These editors spoke directly to the reader, excluding from account anyone else. 'No compromise' was the war cry of Robert Robinson's *Isis*. His May 3, 1950, leader insisted:

> '*The Isis* is not representative in any way of the University at large: if it were, it would be unconscionably dull. It can, if you wish, be regarded as a symbol of the Oxford complexion, just as OUDS or Vincents, or any other of the hoary old institutions may be. And the only end of *The Isis* is to entertain those who read it and those who produce it. Since it doesn't take itself seriously, consider itself significant, permanently valuable; believe itself righteous, moral, decadent or documentary—it finds itself mildly embarrassed when it discovers others hotly concerned for its welfare. And it wishes that those who find indignation to be an indispensable part of living would stick to

vivisection, contraceptives, proportional representation or any of the other famous items in the amazing collection of sociological *trivia*.'

Of course, if a would-be writer found one editor's version of *Isis* insupportable, there was always the chance he would be able to work with the next a term later.

In recent years, national student press competitions have suggested that *Isis* has been overtaken in imagination by the publications of younger universities. What safeguards against permanent decline is the magazine's secret of eternal youth. As journal to Oxford's Shangri-la, *Isis* can never grow old. And it will take only the arrival of another Nichols, Robinson or Potter for it to be changed utterly once more.

What follows is some of the best writing from a few of the most distinguished contributors.

Andrew Billen
Mark Skipworth

Hilaire Belloc's *full name was Joseph Hilaire Pierre Sebastian René Swanton Belloc, though he was known to his Oxford friends as Peter. An 1895* Isis *'Idol' described him as a 'Catholic, artilleryman, journalist, draughtsman, poet, sailing master, etc., etc.' He was also president of the Oxford Union. He died in 1953, and is now perhaps remembered chiefly as a children's writer.*

On Sleep, by a Don (Mr Lambkin, M.A.)

(We have had the inestimable privilege of seeing the advance sheets of Mr Lambkin's new book of essays entitled 'Rictus Almae Matris'. He has given us permission to publish the little gem that follows, and we trust this amiable indiscretion will lead all our readers to give the book the position it deserves, when it appears.)

In Sleep our faculties lie dormant[a]. We perceive nothing or almost nothing of our surroundings; and the deeper our slumber the more absolute is the barrier between ourselves and the outer world. The causes of this 'Cessation of Consciousness' (as it has been admirably called by Professor McObvy[b]) lie hidden from our most profound physiologists. It was once my privilege to meet the master of physical science who has rendered famous the University of Kreigenswald[c], and I asked him what in his opinion was the cause of sleep. He answered, with that reverence which is the glory of the Teutonic mind, 'It is in the dear secret of the All-wise Nature-mother preserved.' I have never forgotten those wise and weighty words[d].

Perhaps the nearest guess as to the nature of Sleep is to be discovered in the lectures of a brilliant but sometimes over-daring young scholar whom we applaud in the chair of Psychology. 'Sleep' (he says) 'is the direct product of Brain-Somnolence, which in its turn is the result of the need for Repose that every organism must experience after any specialized exertion.' I was present when this sentence was delivered, and I am not ashamed to add that I was one of those who heartily cheered the young speaker[e].

We may assert, then, that Science has nearly conquered this last stronghold of ignorance and superstition[f].

As to the Muses, we know well that Sleep has been their favourite theme for ages. With the exception of Catullus (whose verses have been greatly over-rated, and who is always talking of people lying awake at night), all the ancients have mentioned and praised this innocent pastime. Every one who has done Greats will remember the beautiful passage in Lucretius[g], but perhaps that in Sidonious Apollinaris, the highly polished Bishop of Gaul, is less well known[h]. To turn to our own literature, the sonnet beginning 'To die, to sleep', etc.[i], must be noted, and above all, the glorious lines in which Wordsworth reaches his noblest level, beginning—

'It is a pleasant thing to go to sleep!'

lines which, for my part, I can never read without catching some of their magical drowsy influence[j].

All great men have slept. George III frequently slept[k], and that great and good man Wycliffe was in the habit of reading his Scriptural translations and his own sermons nightly to produce the desired effect[l]. The Duke of Wellington (whom my father used to call 'The Iron Duke') slept on a little bedstead no larger than a common man's.

As for the various positions in which one may sleep, I treat of them in my little book of Latin Prose for Schools, which is coming out next year[m].

a. The very word 'dormant' comes from the Latin for 'sleeping'.
b. I knew Professor McO. in the sixties. He was a charming and cultured Scotchman, with a thorough mastery of the English tongue.
c. Dr von Lieber-Augustin. I knew him well. He was a charming and cultured German.
d. How different from the cynical ribaldry of Voltaire!
e. Mr Buffin. I know him well. His uncle is Lord Glenaltamont, one of the most charming and cultured of our new peers.
f. See especially 'Hypnotism', being the researches of the Research Society (xiv. vols., London, 1893) and 'Superstitions of the Past, especially the belief in the influence of Sleep upon Spells', by Dr Beradini. Translated by Mrs Blue. (London, Tooby & Co., 1895).
g. Bk I or Bk IV.
h. 'Amo dormire. Sed nunquam dormio post nonas horas nam episcopus sum et volo dare bonum exemplum fidelibus.' App. Sid. Epistol., Bk III, Epist. 26. (Libermach's edition, Berlin, 1875.) It has the true ring of the fifth century.
i. So Herrick, in his famous epigram on Buggins. A learned prelate of my acquaintance would frequently quote this.
j. The same lines occur in several other poets. Notably *Tupper* and *Montgomery*.
k. See 'Private Memoirs of the Court of Geo. III and the Regent', by Mrs Fitz-H---t.
l. See further, 'The Morning Star of England', in 'Stirrers of the Nations Series', by the Rev. H. Turmsey, M.A. Also 'Foes and Friends of John of Gaunt', by Miss Matchkin.
m. 'Latin Proses', 3s. 6d. net. Jason & Co., Piccadilly.

(November 27, 1897)

Max Beerbohm *was a brilliant satirist and gifted cartoonist, who established himself well before leaving Merton College. He remarked once, 'My gifts are small; I've used them very well and discreetly, never straining them, and the result is that I've made a charming little reputation.' Sir Max died in 1956.*

’ΕΥΔΑΙΜΟΝΙΑ

Smug, in your attic crooning
    Your Aristotle through,
The yellow sun is swooning
    At the sight of you!

You look as though in midnight-oil
    You washed your features sallow;
Dark is your hand with penman's toil;
    Your hair lies fallow.

Look from your window! Down below,
    The fast man flits, divinely clad;—
To him Life's 'clipping, don't you know,'
    And 'not half bad.'

He knows no philosophic plan
    Of Happiness, nor ever will.

The "Smug" and the "Blood."   Drawn by MAX BEERBOHM.

You think him a barbarian?
    So be it! Still,

Sour is your life as sweet is his;
    High spirits and a little money
Are more than all the treatises.
    . . . Isn't it funny?

(*May 28, 1898*)

Philip Guedalla *was President of the Oxford Union and gained a First in Modern History at Balliol. He was acclaimed as a popular historian and also published some verse. He died in 1944.*

Song

I like to hang about the Schools
With all the other silly fools;
I like electric bells that ring
And men who shout like anything;
I like to wear an evening tie
And feel like people do, who die
In railway-carriages abroad
With no communication-cord;
I like the little traps they set,
The seven facts you just forget,
The answer that you cannot quite,
The map you very nearly might,
The final incidence of Tithe,
The Manor of the Soke of Hythe,
The case of *Pennyfeather v.
Commissioners of Treasury*,
The judgment of Trevena J.
Deciding just the other way,
The things that probably were done

In August, 1381,
The points that really mattered to
The men who fought in '92,
The principles that were to be
Significant in '93,
The recent memories that bore
Upon events in '94,
The due proportions of the Hide,
The fact that Benedetti lied,
The ineradicable faults
In renderings of Von der Goltz,
The irremediable gaps
In frankly well-intentioned maps:
These are the kind of thing to please
The men who liked such things as these.

(June 22, 1912)

A. P. Herbert *was an exhibitioner of New College, graduated with a First in Jurisprudence and was later admitted to the bar. Although he never practised, Alan Patrick Herbert's legal knowledge was put to hilarious use in his many books of 'Misleading Cases'. For 15 years he was MP for Oxford before the university seat was abolished. He died Sir Alan in 1971.*

Love Locked In

When I observe the lovelorn minstrel troll
In dismal strains his amorous devotion,
    I feel that he has all the bliss
    (Knowing the necessary Miss),
While I—I simply do not know a soul
Who could inspire me with the least
      emotion.

I long for someone who will fill the gap;
I seek her still, from early youth I've
      sought her.

    At school I nursed a bitter grudge
    Against my master, Mr Budge—
In other ways a very decent chap—

Because he never had a little daughter.
Sometimes I see a damsel in the train,
Or some young goddess in a host of
      dancers,
     Who simply conquers me at sight
     (Like Muriel the other night),
And then—confound!—we never meet
      again;
It's ten to one she cuts me for the Lancers.

I am a very tender-hearted bard,
And gentle thoughts are frequent in my
      chaste head.
     Yes, I could love like fun, but oh!
     I cannot love the girls I know!
Indeed it is exceptionally hard
That all my ardour is completely wasted.

Will no fair lady make the first advance?
I must love somebody or perish shortly.
     You wouldn't like to see me wed
     To some uncomely dame instead.
Well then, secure me while you have the
      chance,
Or you'll regret it when you're old and
      portly.

              (June 22, 1912)

The Inter-war Years

Beverley Nichols, *author, journalist and composer,*
said in 1978 of editing The Isis, *'I obviously had a gift*
for journalism—sometimes I wish I hadn't—and I
simply saw, perhaps in advance of my time, how to edit
The Isis.*'*

The Sad Story of the Young Gentleman from M-rt-n

'I will wear Cubist
Trousers,'
He said.
'I will make Oxford beautiful.
I will make the High
Hectic,
And the Corn
Crimson,' he said.
'I *will* wear Cubist
Trousers.'

However, the Philistines
(Who were not
Beautiful)
Beset him.
'We will not have Cubist
Trousers,' they said.
'It is not nice to wear Cubist

Trousers,'
They said.
'They are affected.
Let us de-
Bag him.'
And they de-
Bagged him.

This is what always happens at Oxford
When one tries
To be
Decorative.

We *will* wear Cubist trousers.

(*April 30, 1919*)

M.

Earnest sat down to read Ruby M. Ayres on the top of the Radcliffe Camera. There was something rather wonderful about reading Ruby M. Ayres on the top of the Radcliffe Camera, like eating bad tomatoes on the top of the Alps. What a wonderful name it was, too—Ruby—well, that was clear enough—she *was* rather that sort of person. Ayres—that was obvious, although the Graces weren't so easy to find. What puzzled him was the M.

He frowned. Four carts whizzed by, far below, carrying carnations to the Co-op. Big Tom boomed three, and the purple tones faded ecstatically into the jade tintinabulations of Trinity College, which struck half-past six. Far away in the distance a dog refused to bark.

Earnest frowned again. What *could* the M. be? What was the use of M. anyhow? It was a distressingly conventional letter—two silly legs and a sort of hiccup in the middle.

A horribly regular letter—it always reminded him of a mantelpiece with two china dogs, exactly alike, at each corner, and two dusty vases, that longed to be filled with aspidestrias, in the middle. Besides, it stood for Mumps and Mauve, and Meat, and Morning. How different from N, now, with its marvellous incompleteness, one leg sticking up in the air, and a slim slanting body, telling of News, and Nepotism, and Narcissus, and Neoplatonism, and Night.

Earnest sighed. This was too tedious. Here he was with trousers fresh from the Clarendon Cleaning Works, underneath a sky that suggested monstrous Things to the gargoyles on the Bodleian, prepared for the eternal moment. It would never recur again. Never again would four carts whiz by carrying carnations to the Co-op. Never again would the sound of big Tom be quite so purple, or the clock at Trinity strike such a jade half-past six. Never again would a dog refuse to bark at just the right moment. And all because of this nasty M.

Now—if it had been Ruby Ayres—well, that would have suggested blood-red incense floating over the roofs of some perfect mediæval city—or if it had been Ruby Mayres, that would have conjured up visions of scarlet horses galloping into the dawn.

'M-m-m,' said Earnest. Far away in the distance a dog barked.

(*October 29, 1919*)

Evelyn Waugh *gained a scholarship to Hertford College where he managed only a Third in History. Dilys Powell remembered him in a large, floppy black bow-tie, riding around Oxford on a fast and noisy motorcycle. His friend Harold Acton said, 'Try as I might I could never acquire Evelyn's taste for beer, but because I delighted in his company I sipped it at his offal luncheons, where everybody talked at once, reciting Edith Sitwell's* Façade *and other poems, and expressing our* joie de vivre. *We were aesthetic hearties.'*

Oxford and the Next War: a letter of exhortation from an undergraduate to a friend abroad.

Dear Bill,
It occurs to me that I have allowed almost the whole term to go by without writing to you. This was disgraceful. My only excuse can be your utter remoteness and the complete heart-breaking dreariness of everyone and everything in Oxford.

You did well to go down. I can think of nothing which has happened this term which could at all interest you. All your friends have behaved more or less abominably to each other, as they used in your time, and have fallen into various degrees of ill favour with the authorities. The Proctors have been perculiarly aggressive this term. You probably saw, or will have seen before you get this, that they banned our 1840 Exhibition without any sort of reason. They seem to be determined that we shall not enjoy ourselves. The other day I was walking home with a pickaxe which I borrowed to complete the costume of 'the Conservative Working Man' for a fancy dress party, when I was stopped by a bowler-hatted servant and brought to the Proctors, who told me that it was not seemly to carry workmen's tools about. I wonder if it was just snobbery or ill-nature, or whether he was afraid of being attacked.

The Union has been sadder than ever and has just been celebrating a centenary. I do think it is time that something was done to stop the thing. You cannot imagine what the debates have been like this term, with Scaife setting a tone of arrogant mediocrity and people like de Gruchy trying to clear things up. They have elected Gerald Gardiner President this term—do you remember him? A tall man with a jerky voice who is generally writing things in the OUDS.

The OUDS, by the way, have shown themselves in no way as contemptuous of the Press as Scaife. I have never seen anything like the amount of comment and praise which Gyles' simple little performance of 'Hamlet' roused in the London papers. It was a thoroughly good amateur show; that is to say, everyone knew his part tolerably well, and the lights didn't go out or the curtains catch fire, or the wigs come off, or anything like that, but all the fuss in Fleet Street was utterly silly. It is a pity that all these editors and reporters treat Oxford so seriously. They even, some of them, swallowed poor Jim Fagan's lame little excuses about 'infinity' for his very commonplace 'geometry and curtains'.

The Bicester have had to close down owing to foot-and-mouth disease, but that doesn't affect a poor man like myself. There has been quite enough to exasperate us all without that.

You know, Bill, what we want is another war. I become more and more convinced of that every day.

These tiresome historians always find causes for their wars in national expansion and trade rivalry and religion and such things. I don't know about these because, as you know, I am never up in time to read the newspapers, but I gather from those who do that things are pretty unsettled. What seems to me more important is that we have a great body of young men of all sorts of education just longing for another general disturbance. We all had the fortune to be brought up in easy familiarity with bombs and casualty lists and bad bread and all the things young men used to be warned about, and we know exactly how bearable and unbearable they are.

We also know that when there is a war the fighting people at least have moments of really intense enjoyment and really intense misery—both things which one wants at our age. As far as I can see, there is just no chance of any of us being able to earn a living decent enough to allow of any sort of excitement or depravity. Here we are with bills, overfastidious tastes, and a completely hopeless future. What can we do but to long for a war or a revolution?

If on your travels you meet any traitors who want to levy war against the king, or kings who want to overthrow representative institutions, or fanatics who want to convert people by the sword to some ghastly religion, or jolly adventurers who want to kill all the Mormons or check the Yellow Peril, or restore the Hapsburgs or the Stuarts, or invade America in the cause of alcohol or China in the cause of opium, or France in the cause of Sabbatarianism, or the Vatican in the cause of compulsory vaccination, please tell them, him or her that we can raise a very jolly platoon of gentlemen-adventurers for them in Oxford if they, he or she will pay us handsomely and give us a good chance of a speedy death.

What a long letter, Bill!

Yours,

EVELYN

(*March 12, 1924*)

The Union

I did not think that it was a good debate on Thursday. I have always noticed that there is nothing like a discussion on education for bringing out all that is most priggish and silly in

46

people. The pietism of Mr Matthews, Mr Monkhouse's love of the beauty of youth, the simple snobbery of the Teller for the Ayes—all, I must admit, wearied me a good deal.

Not that all the speeches were bad. Mr Matthews was, as always, extremely smooth and efficient, and Mr Lloyd-Jones extraordinarily interesting. But I do think that we had a worse debate than we had a right to expect; after all it was a subject upon which we all had first-hand knowledge.

The motion was, 'That immediate and very drastic reforms are needed in our so-called Public Schools.'

In the absence of Mr Bernays, it was moved by Mr I. B. Lloyd (Exeter). He had had only two hours in which to prepare his speech, and so he may well be excused for his only fault—that he had nothing new to say. He made all the usual criticisms about class feeling, the original intentions of the founders of the grammar schools, the inefficiency of the curriculum, the new order of society which had no place for a governing class, and so on. It was all very orthodox, but we had heard it before, Mr Lloyd!

Mr P. J. Monkhouse (Trinity) was not a buffoon until after his speech. About public schools he felt very seriously and very sentimentally. Socially a public school was a city state—a stage of civilisation through which one should pass in order to gain a full development; aesthetically it was 'a great light and beauty'. The only criticism which he would make was that there should be more schools and cheaper schools, so that all classes might go there.

Mr R. de C. Matthews spoke third. To be honest, I was a little disappointed by him, not because he was not by far the best of the speakers on paper and indeed, with one exception, of all the speakers that evening, but because one has learned to expect really good oratory and really able satire from him. On Thursday he made a smooth, almost an unctuous, debating speech, but I felt that he was not doing himself justice. He spoke of the serious nature of marriage, and how ill one was prepared for it by a public school; he explained what his ideal man was like, and showed that public school men were not like that. I think that he is better on a frankly political motion.

Mr H. A. McClure Smith is an honest conservative, and he defended public schools with a certain glibness. Either he or

Mr Matthews, I cannot from my notes decide which, said that the worst characteristic of Englishmen was their facility for tolerating bad institutions as good jokes. I thought that amusing. I think Mr Matthews must have said it.

Mr Evelyn Waugh was guilty of a breach of good manners, for which he is sorry.

Mr A. R. Burn (Christ Church) thought the public schools an agreeable illusion and an embryo πόλις. I am not quite sure what he meant, but I liked his speech.

Mr M. A. Franklin (Queen's) talked some vulgar and rather irrelevant nonsense about co-education.

Mr A. E. Hill (St Edmund Hall) delivered a well-prepared eulogy of the Oundle experiment, whatever that may be.

The only really fine speech of the evening was made by Mr Lloyd-Jones (Jesus). I admire this speaker more every time I hear him. He has the sense not to be ashamed of being earnest about things, never aims at effect and always achieves it. He denounced public schools as breaking up family life. It was a point which in many discussions I have not heard raised before. I was sorry that no one combated it all the evening.

Mr Gyles Isham wants to have mediaeval Latin taught. He said that he intended to be 'frank' about school morals, but he wasn't particularly.

Mr A. H. E. Molson didn't want a good character. He resented change. He thought French schools worse than his.

Mr F. P. Streeton was the gentleman who wanted a good character. He also, I thought, wanted a sense of humour. Still, he made a pretty effective attack on schools for their discipline, military training, compulsory chapel, etc. He seemed to me to have rather a feminine point of view towards things.

Mr Alfonso de Zulueta (New College) made a jolly maiden speech. He began badly but soon got clearer, and told an enchanting story about a school where the matron was wanton.

Mr J. Dugdale (Christ Church) wanted to have the masters taught.

Mr W. L. Somers (Magdalen) made the same criticism that you couldn't cut down the expenses of education. As it was the masters were second-rate enough.

48

Mr J. L. Parker (New College) was rather ingenious.

Mr J. R. Sutro (Trinity) was very amusing. Rugby had taught him hatred of English cooking. He was not sick.

Mr D. Neylan (Trinity) showed that exercise and games were not exchangeable terms.

Mr S. F. Villiers-Smith (New College) made the sort of speech which one associates with aged colonels. He used all the heavy phrases about 'making a chap toe the line'; he resented 'all this talk about individuality'. I thought it sad to find anyone talking like that at Mr Smith's age.

Mr N. Wylie (Keble) thought it would help if they taught agriculture.

Mr Nobbs (Wadham) actually used the expression, 'made the Empire what is is.'

Mr R. P. S. Wadds (Balliol) had been to three schools in three countries. They were all alike; therefore they were good. A strange argument.

Mr A. L. Ungoed-Jones (Magdalen) thought schools were there to turn out placid folk.

Mr D. E. G. Kennard (New College) made a little fun about the ideal day at the ideal school. He had been to Eton; the chief value of public schools was to make 'gentlemen'.

Mr Pares closed the debate delightfully.

There voted:—Ayes, 15; Noes, 108.

(May 22, 1924)

Harold Acton *was an undergraduate at Christ Church where he is said to have painted his rooms bright yellow. An* Isis *'Idol' noted, 'Mr Acton always attracts attention by sheer distinction of manner while eschewing the eccentricities by which lesser men seek to make themselves conspicuous.' Today the historian and critic lives in Florence, where he was born in 1904.*

Byron and the Recent Centenary

I do not like Centenaries. They dole out to every journalist-prattler an excuse for talking an infinite deal of opaque generalisations about the dead, who, as we all know, are deprived of the estimable capacity to retort, or of the conventional comedy-wife's prerogative, to get the last sheer word. How Byron would have despised them; how he would squirm, could he but hear the little prying nobodies manufacturing puling newspaper-columns and paragraphs out of the splendid raw-material of his name, his love-affairs, and those essential thoughts and emotions which he has transmitted, with so magnificent a gesture, to the centuries!

Centenaries neither lead to beauty nor to majesty: they are the bastards of that modern advertising process, which is doing its utmost to poison the few surviving veins that convey pure ruby blood into the dessicated, palsied, and crumbling members of humanity. They lead inevitably to that stultification of the intellect, which results in Mr Huxley's arrogant formula: 'I glory in the name of ear-wig.'

The universe exists for the purpose of the soul—a fact which has, alas, never been realised by these frolicsome centenary-celebrators. They would as soon commemorate Ella Wheeler Wilcox and Marie Corelli. But there are centenaries and centenaries.

The recent one connected with the name of Byron has succeeded in rehabilitating his character with the prudes, and in relieving it of many Nonconformist prejudices, but it will not alter the opinion of the few who really matter, the few who are not afraid of wit, independence and rebelliousness, who understand his fatigues and his disillusions, and who do not flinch at the intensity of his scourge and the pungency and power of his large loose philippics.

If Byron were at a university such as Oxford today, the Proctors would no doubt treat him as a corrupt influence, and all the stiff-collared professors and myopic searchers after the heel-less slipper Truth who now edit and deface his poems with irrelevant and pedantic annotations, would sneer at their youthfulness in the *Oxford Magazine*.

Even the memory of Missolonghi, which to many minds excused and explained the complexities of Byron's character, would not dispel the evil aroma which that odious paragon of venom and mediocrity, Mrs Harriet Beecher Stowe, sprinkled like incense about his name. But this incense was bound to be sprinkled, as in the case of Oscar Wilde, over one whose fate, as he himself predicted, was to be 'hurt by admiration and imitation'.

Was Byron merely the 'lord who condescended to be a poet'? On this question hangs the pendulum of Byron's aesthetic worth. To be sure, the amateur is common enough in English Literature. As Mr Lytton Strachey exclaimed: 'How many of the greatest English writers would have denied that they were men of letters! Scott, Byron, Gray, Sir Thomas Browne, perhaps even Shakespeare himself.' One remembers Voltaire's disgust when Congreve requested him to address him as a gentleman rather than as a writer, and then Sainte-Beuve's: '*Si vous estimez la Poésie un trop petit sujet pour vous, laissez-la tranquille.*' But Byron's extreme fervour, and the facility with which he testified it, confirm the unfairness of the gibe.

It is so easy, so superficial, to remark with Carlyle that Byron was a dandy unacquainted with grief. This species of observation may go down well over the tea-cups at some Shepherd's Bush literary society, and I can visualize the delight with which the Early Victorians licked their chops over so luscious a phrase, imagining, perhaps, that they were enjoying a 'religious awakening'—but it were more advisable to slumber on in ignorance and bliss than to hearken to the Evangelist and High Church manifestations of bogey-men—as they have since been established.

Like all the Romantics, like Goethe, de Musset, Wordsworth, Manzoni, Byron suffered intensely—despite his florid rhetoric and a copiousness which often becomes wearisome. But it was only when in 'Don Juan' he came to Gissing's conclusion that we only live our lives by laughing a little in the presence of suffering that 'the pulse of vital blood felt in tangible flesh' found a medium of expression with the potency of true Genius, and this Byron is not the *milord anglais* whom the world adores and over whose remains and souvenirs the centenary-celebrators have been gibbering, as Nubian witch-doctors over some new-discovered spell. Their Byron, American in his energy, is the tireless exponent of corsairs and giaours, their wiles and wickedness, their lurid perpetual passions and petulant partialities. Their Byron, like Rupert Brooke, is mainly doted on for the comeliness of his features and his rather fascinating lack of control. They have invested in this Byron as in gilt-edged securities. He has mellowed as old port. They feel he is thoroughly safe, *almost* respectable, in fact. ('A bit of a lad with the gals, some bird, by Jove, what, what?' with a readjustment of the monocle.) But the anarchic master of the Satanic School might be dead as a door-nail, so far as they are concerned. He might not exist. He is gone with the nightmare drawings of Fuseli and the vast decorative panels of Benjamin Robert Haydon. He has become the pathetic *enfant terrible* of vicarage-libraries, where a few elderly maidens, exuding a faint odour of camphor and Cranford, shudder over 'Parisina'.

(May 7, 1924)

Dilys Powell *was suspended for two terms in her final year for climbing into Somerville late one night, but nevertheless gained a First in French. She remembers* The Isis *as 'little more than a nuisance, an irresponsible undergraduate frolic, not at all a serious attempt at journalism'. Film critic on the* Sunday Times, *she wrote for* The Isis *on general topics, even though there was a cinema page at the time.*

Which Freedom?

'*Beauty crieth in an attic and no man regardeth*'—Samuel Butler

There was once a respectable middle-class man who had three daughters. The eldest was pretty and rather active; she was educated at a boarding-school where she acquired music and deportment; and when she came to years of indiscretion she flirted so successfully that she captured a well-to-do oil merchant and lived with him in indolence for the rest of her days. The second daughter was full of common sense and the soul of efficiency; she received a sound modern education at a high school, where she made herself so invaluable that the monitorial system tottered and almost fell at her departure. She decided early in life not to marry, and took a post as secretary to a women's organisation. But the youngest daughter was different from the other two. She had a great longing for independence, and having studied the progress of her sisters she decided that neither of them had achieved it. She did not herself propose to pander to the caprice and preside over the plutocratic dinner-table of an oil merchant; nor did she intend to prove her dependence on the opposite sex by ostentatiously segregating herself from it and conducting Feminist campaigns against it. She therefore resolved, on leaving school, that a University education would best meet her requirements; for in a University, she had been given to understand, women, whilst being independent of masculine whims, yet met men on terms of friendship and equality. She hoped that in this atmosphere, by taking advantage of the many and varied interests Oxford affords, she might equip herself for the battle of life and train herself as a woman and not as an animal or a machine.

Having arrived at her college, she proceeded to put her plans into execution. Her work, she felt, could develop fully only if she herself developed intellectually in as many directions as possible; she therefore did not stint the hours spent at literary, musical, and dramatic societies, nor did she scorn the pursuit of subjects other than her own. She had not reckoned, however, with her tutors. One day the overseer of her studies summoned her and asked her if it were true that in the same term she was both singing in the Bach Choir Festival and acting in her college play. The girl replied in the affirmative; whereupon her tutor, declaring that such a state of affairs would be detrimental to her work, decreed that this must not be; and neither blandishments nor tears had power to move her. And so the girl went away sorrowing; for she had learnt that her college was a place, not of education, but of hard labour.

But she was not discouraged; for, she said to herself, 'although one's intellectual development is dependent on the caprice of women, one is at least on an equal and friendly footing with men.' And so she borrowed a pencil from the undergraduate next to her at a lecture, and he wheeled her bicycle to her college gate. A few days later, however, she learned from the lips of her Principal that though a few minutes' chat with an undergraduate was allowed, longer conversations between lectures were contrary to the regulations of the University. On enquiring the cause of this she was informed that it was important not to give PEOPLE any opportunity for ill-natured gossip about the women students. (It seemed it did not matter about the men.) For the same reason, apparently, it was essential that if, after 7 p.m., a body of young men entered a womens' college for the purpose of debating on the British Empire or a kindred subject, the Principal's permission for the intrusion should be obtained. On learning this the girl sighed and grew despondent; for if both chats and debates damaged the reputation of a college there could be little stability in it.

Still her spirit was not broken; for, she told herself, though one might be shut in from the intellectual and artistic life in Oxford—though one might be allowed to regard the opposite sex only through the grill of propriety —one could still see quite a lot. And thinking that out of term at least she was free, she promised the undergraduate whose pencil she had borrowed to go with him to a Commemoration Ball. It was with distress that when, as was demanded by her college authorities, she gave notice that she desired to remain in Oxford after term, and supplied her reason for this extraordinary whim, she learned that even here she must conform to various regulations. She could not, said her Principal, sleep in her college on the night of the ball, for the porter would be abed and unable to admit her; and on the girl objecting that she had no wish to sleep anywhere, since the revels continued until 6 a.m., she rejoined that lest illness should overtake her she must have an address. This, however, was not all; for, said the Principal, if she knew no Oxford lady resident who would house her and sign a form promising not to give her a latch-key, she must have her mother stay with her in lodgings and give the same promise.

Now the girl's mother had been divorced and not heard of these fifteen years; so the girl bethought her that a Commemoration Ball gave more trouble than it was worth; and she did not stay to hear that a chaperone was necessary, but went away abruptly. And the next day she packed her belongings and left the University; 'for,' she said, 'I had best go down before I be sent.'

(June 4, 1924)

Claud Cockburn, *a student of Keble College, not only edited* The Isis *but wrote a column for one of the Oxford city papers. He became an outstanding radical journalist, editing the notorious newsheet* The Week *in the Thirties, and contributing to* Private Eye *until his death in 1981.*

Experience

You say you were at Euston Station on Monday evening? Well, I was the man who got arrested. (And I may as well tell you, dear, dear reader, if you *were* there, that I didn't at all like the way you gaped at me on that occasion. Lots of great men have been imprisoned. Look at Napoleon, and all the Russian novelists.) Not that I care. It was an experience. If I fall into debt, or in the river; when I am a prey to the sad conviction that I have tipped the Barabbas at that Belgian hotel too little, or the even sadder conviction that I have tipped him too much, 'This,' I say to myself, 'is an experience, and will no doubt prove profitable.'

At present I am a prey to a conviction for petty larceny. Possibly it was the result of travelling all day from the North, and pulling out at once on the old underground train to Victoria. For 'men bulk large on the west trail, our own trail, the old trail, the trail that is always new'. They bulked particularly large in my carriage that evening, especially on that section of the trail that one hits at Charing Cross, and it was only at Victoria that I had room to notice the feeling that I was carrying less than I had been when I stuck in the doorway of the carriage at Euston, and delayed five eager Scotsmen for nearly three minutes in their southward trek to the premier-ship.

The feeling was justified—it always is—and in a few minutes I was hurrying back to Euston not at all rejoicing in the numberless overcoats and travelling-rugs I carried, and still less in the one attaché case that had gone astray. I have always understood that Euston Station is a home from home for the pickpocket and the crook. There's something about the air of the place that suits them wonderfully. If you stop bewaring of them for a moment they rush out and rob you. The road going down from Jerusalem to Jericho isn't, so to speak, in the same street with the lanes round Euston. Judge, then, of my amazement when I saw the attaché case standing on the kerb at the top of Number One platform.

I hurried towards it, and then hesitated. The fact is I don't look nearly as honest as my terror of the police forces me to be. Suppose people took me for a crook? The great thing was to avoid any appearance of slinking. I stood quite still beside the case and lit a cigarette. Surely no crook would do that? Then, 'The thief conducted the robbery with the most brazen-faced assumption of unconcern,' I remembered reading somewhere. People were staring at me! Good heavens! I was being bewared of! Regretfully recollecting the dotted lines—never, alas! cut along by me—of coupons advertising 'blushing cured in three lessons', I picked up the case and sauntered off. There was a policeman. Good. I would have a little chat with him. 'Lots of people travelling—er officer?' I said cheerily.

'Sir?'

When he said 'Sir?' like that I wished I'd said something more repeatable, something of more permanent worth. It was like rushing up to Dean Inge and telling him you thought it was going to rain. I just said, 'Well-Imeantersayeh?' and to my horror found myself actually slinking away. Inside the tube entrance I breathed as freely as my burdens permitted. It's ridiculous, I thought, to be so upset. 'After all,' I said aloud, 'it's my own bag.' 'That's just where you're wrong,' said a nasty voice behind me. 'Thought you'd got away with it, eh?' I turned round and faced my policeman and an unkind-looking man. I grasped at once that this was what my inexpensive and wise morning paper calls a situation—almost, indeed, a crisis. The atmosphere was far from friendly. Obviously it was the moment to make a gesture. But I'm not a very good statesman, and the other fellow did it first, pointing acquisitively at the initials on the attaché case, which were almost incredibly different from my own. I went very quietly indeed.

(December 3, 1924)

Graham Greene *edited the literary magazine* Oxford Outlook *and published a book of verse while he was at Balliol. He met Evelyn Waugh, probably through Waugh's cousin Claud Cockburn. Waugh recorded his impression that Greene 'looked down on us . . . as childish and ostentatious. He certainly shared in none of our revelry'. On leaving he became a sub-editor on* The Times.

Fragment from 'Angina Pectoris': A Long Poem

'But Doctor,' he was saying in his sleep,
And turned a petulant head upon the pillow;
'But Doctor, any day?—a cry, a fall,
Surfeit of food, a bath too hot—
And once I thought to end with dignity,
A trumpet crying out behind the hill,
Wet feet that pass through murmuring meadow grass,
A little smoke that drafts across the moon . . .
And now perhaps go guzzled to my God,
With too many oysters for the heart to hold,
And vomit out upon the glassy sea.
He woke when the sun swept through the yellow holland
To make a candle of his turned-up nose,
And leave a halo round the hyacinths.
He breathed again in a glorious relief,

Whispering 'It was a dream and it is over.'
Then sick again and trembling in the head,
'It was a dream, that's true.' So he lay long.
There seemed no reason why he should arise,
And choose tie, socks, traditional shoes.
If he lay still and quiet, did not stir
Even to wipe the moisture from his nose,
He might live longer by a score of hours,
Twelve hundred minutes, seconds uncountable—
And oh, that strip of light across the room.
The notes came dancing up the golden stair,
Ginked lengthways at him with pencilled, pin-point eyes,
Took his applause, contemptuously were gone,
A bird was singing in the elder tree.
A bee beat buzzing up against the pane.

(June 3, 1925)

Philip Magnus *entered the Civil Service after leaving Wadham College. A historical biographer, Sir Philip's most famous works include biographies of Raleigh, Kitchener, King Edward VII and Gladstone.*

Sonnet on Westminster Bridge

(*As re-composed by one of the ultra-modern school*)

The terrestial pudding hath nothing to absolutely show
    more extravagant.
  Void would he be of guts, a very vacuum among
    mortals, who could stagger past
  A spectacle more Napoleonic in its waywardness.
The city now wears, like an intimate garment of wool,
The beatitude of the forenoon; naked, exposed,
  Stray cats, lost dogs, Houses of Parliament, boats,
    beetles and Big Ben lie
      Under the sky—
All most utterly damnable, and set off by the reeking river
  plastered with stinking scum.

Never did solar ball in a fashion more inexplicable dye
  With his own patent the rotting corpses of rats at low
    water.
I declare I never felt so deeply moved before in my life.

The river goes bowling along as it pleases.
My God! even the wretches on the embankment seem
    asleep,
  And, bless my soul! I've got to be at the office at nine
    o'clock.

(January 20, 1926)

John Betjeman, *who was appointed Poet Laureate in 1972, was sent down from Magdalen College before he could take his degree. A tutor told him he would have received only a Third. His Oxford days are described in his verse biography* Summoned by Bells. *'Our Lovely Lodging-houses!' is the only signed piece Sir John wrote for* The Isis.

Our Lovely Lodging-houses!

Let us open that yellow 'grained oak' front door whose upper panels of stained glass foretell what may be ecclesiastical within. The clouds of Irish stew make the gloom more impenetrable and the elaborate bamboo umbrella-stand more emphatic than ever. Clutching the rather greasy knob of the pitch pine bannisters, we ascend to the front room.

Two ill-proportioned staring plate-glass windows gape at the Gothico-Norman architecture of the red and grey brick houses opposite, framed in coffee-coloured lace curtains neatly looped with pale blue ribbon. The interspace of the windows contains a lithograph of our Lord on one of the mountains around Palestine. Its colours are dimmed by the begonias and roses in a reddish-brown relief on a green background which constitute the wallpaper. Although its floral effect may be interesting, even valuable, this paper does not serve to lighten the room. However, it forms a good set-off for the more prominent feature, the chimney-piece. The grate is framed in richly-coloured tiles and an unobtrusive mantelpiece is hung with red cloth fringed with bobbles and draped in semicircles.

Indeed may the landlady be proud of the overmantel which surmounts the slab. It is a Jacobean-classical structure which wriggles its way to the ceiling shooting out mirrors and brackets left and right and terminating in a debased broken pediment that nibbles the insignificant plaster cornice. And what a wealth of art this overmantel holds! The upper brackets, supported on pillars like stretched sweets, are riddled with Goss china in the form of ships, swans and lighthouses emblazoned with the arms of Whitby, Leamington and Ashton-under-Lyne; the lower brackets contain vases for a single carnation in the irreproachable manner of the 'eighties and little 'quaint' brass figures which betray a later stage of artistic development. The central mirror on the mantel itself reflects a black cat calendar for 1924 and a goo-goo baby doll that were given by a former undergraduate tenant to the landlady, together with the two Bonzo pictures on the east wall.

Of the other furniture of the room little may be said. A slender stand of deal, after an Edwardian design, supports a beaten copper bowl from which flops a magnificent aspidistra. A cupboard into which nothing will fit is painted black and picked out in gold; it supports a fumed oak bookshelf in the Elliston and Cavell manner. The pictures—photographs and oleographs—are either sacred or military. The chairs have sweetly pretty red, yellow and olive green covers and are of beech after an 1890 Jacobean-Rococco-Gothic design.

To an undergraduate who is in the least susceptible to hideousness, this compulsory residence will prove so restless that he cannot work in it, or else it will eat into his very soul, so that an overmantel is a thing to be tolerated—even liked. He cannot move the furniture for fear of offending the landlady, had he the money to buy new. It would, surely, not be difficult to make it compulsory for landladies to put up plain papers, to remove overmantels and aspidistras, and gradually to replace all their furniture with something unobtrusive, were it even 'arts and crafts'.

But no. That brings us even more horrible vistas . . . I can imagine a landlady getting a mania for art cushions and craft salt-cellars . . . the first bright yellow and black, the second unpourable but well meaning . . . Ugh! Then there would be orange-coloured napkins draped over the electric light. And as for calendars—well, a black cat is one thing, but a fabulous beast with art feet and craft tail is indisputably another. We could never stand all that. For at least, now, we are stimulated by the horror of what we see. We are not slowly and insidiously having our mentalities gutted by the atrocious abortions of feeble-minded young ladies working in community schools.

So it's a bad business, whatever happens. Surely the powers that be are under obligation to us to see that something is done?

Oh, YOU DELEGATES OF LODGINGS—STIR YOURSELVES! Or are you a council of landladies?

(October 27, 1926)

Cecil Day Lewis *was born in Ireland, the son of a clergyman. He went to Wadham College where he edited the anthology* Oxford Poetry *in 1927. After working as a schoolmaster, he abandoned teaching for writing. He was made Poet Laureate in 1968, and died in 1976. In 1980 Sean Day Lewis published* Cecil Day Lewis: An English Literary Life.

Hedge-Scholarship

> *Do I contradict myself?*
> *Very well, then, I contradict myself.*
> *(I am large, I contain multitudes.)–Walt Whitman*

When Nature plays hedge-schoolmaster,
　Shakes out the gaudy map of summer
And shows me charabanc, rose, barley-ear
　And every bright-winged hummer;
　To sweat after some revelation

　He asks—the wise old dominie—
　No more of me than, breathing in
This summer scene, to absorb the geography
　Of life and human kin.

But I must needs unleash my brain
   To sweat after some revelation
Behind the rose, heedless if Truth maintain
   On the rose-bloom her station.

Say I, 'The general scheme entails
   Each creature having a like share:
Newt and colossus in the cosmic scales
   Must balance to a hair.

When Fancy conjures with the mist,
   Shaping from it a Danaë's lover,
It proves that in each thing's title to exist
   All titles we discover.
   Yet is the pale ambition, that groups
   One moment and dies in darkness, planned
On the same tragic scale as full-rigged hopes
   Foundering in sight of land?

Reason may say, "The vital spark
   Homuncule with homuncule tallies";
But is it Reason that rates my bank-clerk
   Peer of god-like Achilles?'

Charabancs shout along the lane
   And summer gales bay in the trees
No less superbly because I can't explain
   The essence of their degrees.

Let Logic analyse the hive;
   Wisdom's content to have the honey:
So I'll go bite the crust of life and thrive
   While hedgerows all are sunny.

(November 17, 1926)

Osbert Lancaster, *who later drew his upper-crust cartoons for the* Daily Express, *scraped a now extinct fourth class degree at Lincoln College. He acted at the university and became a friend of John Betjeman.*

Seen in the George: Caricatures

MR. TH-- D -R- Y - T - S.

Mr. J-ck J-rd-n.

Mr. M-lc-lm Y--ng.

(May, 1928)

Michael Foot *made his first speech at the Oxford Union in October 1931. It took him just four terms to become president, following in the footsteps of his two brothers. An* Isis *'Idol' said of the then Liberal Foot that he was 'an uncompromising Radical'. It added, 'He hates the jingoism which he attributes to the Tories as much as he dislikes the attack on individual liberty which he believes to be inherent in socialism, but he never sneers at the views of his opponents.'*

The Rooseveltian Touch

A democracy, no less than a dictatorship, depends for its survival on the calibre of the men who place themselves at its head. Peculiar dangers, it is true, threaten a dictatorial system. There is always a likelihood that Oliver Cromwell may be followed by Tumble-down-Dick. Louis XIV may be succeeded by Louis XV. But democracy too may fail through the incapacity of its leaders.

It may be argued that the world's strong men have been as ineffective as the despised politicians in dealing with our economic problems. Fascist Italy is imposing economy cuts at the moment at which democratic Britain chooses to restore them. But the electorate cannot be relied upon to respond to this appeal to sweet reason. The failure of economic nationalism to remove our difficulties will not prevent Fascists from advocating a full-blooded application of its doctrines. Small doses have proved poisonous. Yet its prescription as a regular diet will find favour. If whips have failed there will be a demand to try scorpions.

It is clear, therefore, that constitutional government will survive, if at all, on its own merits, not on the demerits of opposing systems. It is not sufficient to depict the horrors of despotism. A more positive appeal is required. Democracy is on trial; although qualified to appear as plaintiff, it is cast in the role of defendant.

Thus, the real menace to democracy comes from the possibility of a dearth in its stock of great men. Hero-worship is a well-nigh universal instinct, and in politics it has a vital part to play. It is an instinct which dictators the world over have known how to kindle and enflame. The question whether our present politicians can arouse the same enthusiasm is not a mere idle speculation. It closely concerns the future of democracy.

Certainly something of the glamour has gone out of English politics in the last few years. It may be too much to expect that the rivalry of a Pitt and a Fox, or a Gladstone and a Disraeli should occur more than once in a century. Yet in the competition which they have had to face from film stars and football favourites, our modern politicians have pitiably failed. Of how many of our present-day rulers could it not be said, as Rosebery said of an earlier administration, 'They were good men according to their lights; it is only to be regretted that the men were dull and the lights were dim'? English radicalism, in particular, seems to have lost something of its fire. Effective English Liberalism has always come as a response to dynamic leadership. It was said of John Bright that he would have been a prizefighter had he not been a Quaker; Gladstone only associated himself with the left when he discovered his capacity to move great popular audiences. Modern Socialism with all its reliance on a class-war appeal can present nothing so spectacular as Lloyd George's campaign against the peers and the landowners. Each of these great radical leaders knew the technique of an appeal to the imagination. And it was in 1846, 1870 and 1910 that radicalism celebrated its great triumphs. The art of the orator and the capacity for statesmanship are more closely allied than our technocrats and business politicians would have us think.

This was the weapon which our radical forebears used with such effect to stir the masses from their natural Tory inertia. Modern democrats have let it rust in their hands. And most dangerous of all, their opponents have fashioned implements of a similar pattern for their own purposes. Hitler and Mussolini, the enemies of democracy, are the greatest exponents of demagogy. In modern times those who have wished to oppress the people have learnt to ape the gestures and accents of those who were accustomed to lead them. Every dictator is also a tribune; and the business of propaganda has been exalted into a department of State.

A recent historian has told us that there was one question uppermost in Napoleon's mind: 'What is Paris saying?' The greatest soldier and legislator of all time was probably the greatest journalist. Post-war imitators have not been slow to learn the potentialities of this last profession. The art of modern despotism largely consists of a capacity to satisfy momentary passions at the expense of deep-seated needs. Demagogism is the homage which dictatorship pays to democracy.

Thus if success is to be achieved there is precept in the past and competition in the present to reveal to modern radicalism what is required of it. But only one great democratic leader has made any serious attempt to counteract the appeal to the passions which Fascism successfully achieves. If Hitler asserts that he is creating a New Germany, President Roosevelt is equally aggressive in his claim that he is the leader of a New America.

It is not necessary to outdo the dictators in the megaphone methods which they are compelled to introduce. The salutes, the uniforms and the drilling are appeals to the crudest of all political instincts; they are not necessarily the most powerful. The mock heroics of Goering have already provided a theme for the cartoonist in Berlin. And the mobilisation of professional thugs in this country will continue to cause amusement, unless Disaffection Bills persuade the people that plots to overturn the State are being hatched in every garret in London's underworld. Democracies still possess a great asset which they should hasten to realise. The sense of humour of a nation will always range itself against those statesmen who cultivate prominent jaws and exaggerated scowls. It is no accident that America's great democratic leader should be known to the world with a smile on his face.

President Roosevelt has mastered the art of a democratic appeal in the twentieth century; and our own democratic leaders should learn the lesson which he has to teach. The old weapons have been sharpened to suit a new political warfare. The election slogans, 'the New Deal' and the 'forgotten man', were known throughout the length and breadth of the land. The radio has been exploited to the full for the first time. And the actions of the President in office have revealed once again the dual functions of a great radical leader. An expert window-dresser, he has also shown himself able to sell the right goods across the counter.

The future of democracy in America lies in the President's hands. Few will doubt that his action in the panic-stricken days when he entered office saved that democracy from a complete collapse. Yet his recovery programme was initiated and advertised not by a refusal to let opposing opinions raise their voice, but by a resort to the old radical method of an appeal to a nation's imagination. It is the Rooseveltian touch which will alone rekindle English radicalism.

(May 17, 1934)

Airey Neave *was wounded and taken prisoner by the Nazis while serving with the Territorial Army in France in 1940, but escaped two years later. He went on to write spy novels. A close friend of Mrs Thatcher and a Conservative MP, he was killed by a terrorist bomb outside Parliament in 1979.*

Cake

The rain was falling heavily outside. From her seat in the window Hilde gloomily watched the detachments as they marched by singing and laughing. They were young and handsome, yet Hilde hated and despised them. She was sick to death of hearing the stamping of heavy boots and the ostentatious clicking of heels. She was tired and frightened of their shouting, bullying, manners. Everywhere was this dismal sameness—uniforms, ideas, everything. The paradise that Germany had been promised eighteen months ago seemed further away than ever.

Hans, her lover, would come soon. He was a sculptor, a very intelligent and promising man he had been considered. Before the Revolution he had been making enough for them to be married some day. But his grandmother had been of Jewish extraction. Now he lived in a dim little room and earned a few marks making theatrical masks. Hilde thought of him and cursed the sacred Führer. The marching continued steadily through the rain. In the distance a small figure was approaching with a bundle of books under his arm, saluting every separate detachment as was the law. The girl saw him, as he drew near the house and waved. Hans looked up and smiled wanly. He had had a hard but fruitless day's work. So fixed was his attention on the girl in the window that he walked along regardless of the marching Nazis. He did not notice the passing of a new detachment with its banner. He failed to give the salute. Hilde heard the leader give an angry snarl as he strode up to Hans and accused the poor man of contempt of the glorious flag of his country and the followers of Hitler. The blond men shouted something about taking him to a Kontzentrazionslage. But their leader was in a hurry. He hit Hans hard on the nose so that he reeled, with the blood streaming from where his broken spectacles had cut him. He hit him again on the jaw until he fell and with his head on the pavement. The coarse, animal laugh of the storm-troopers rang in Hilde's ears as they marched on through the rain.

After Hans' death, Hilde could not leave her home for several weeks. She sat by the window all day. Always she seemed to see before her that pathetic figure on the pavement below with his books and papers strewn around him. At last the time came when she felt she must try to forget and earn some money. One day she heard of a vacant post of attendant in the office of the Gruppen-Führer. The thought of it filled her with anger and shame. She could not work with the people who had killed Hans. Suddenly she thought of something else which made her heart beat fast with mingled fear and excitement. A week later she began to work.

Her duties were not arduous, merely scrubbing and polishing and occasionally taking tea and refreshments to the iron-jawed men who worked there. Yet she hated the place and everything to do with it, not only because of Hans but because of the bullying Prussianism of the officers there. Life was hell because she was pretty and they molested her. But she stayed on because she felt in her desperate, distraught way that the time might come when Hans should be avenged.

One afternoon some months later she was crying in the small pantry of the office. A particularly unpleasant member of the staff had been unusually tiresome. He liked her smooth fair hair parted down the middle, and that rather lost, winsome look which is so typical of her type. She had fled from him and decided to go away as soon as she could. Then something happened which made her change her whole attitude towards the office and its staff. Strasser, one of the least repulsive men there, had come in and tried to console her by reading out of the paper.

'You see that man there, Biedermann? Why, he used to be only a plain S.A. man a short time ago, and now he's very important. I knew him well. He was stationed here, but he had some row with a Jew in the street which had to be hushed up. It doesn't seem to have hindered his career. He's going to visit us next Saturday, having mittagessen with the Gruppenführer. Why, you've fainted, Hilde!'

All that week Hilde thought of the face of Biedermann which she had seen in the street hardly a year since. Her chance came on Friday, when she had almost given up hope. She was told that all members of the staff were to join in the general celebrations and pay great respect to Herr Biedermann.

On Saturday afternoon the great man and his comrades were celebrating in the office when there was a knock at the door, and Hilde came in.

'Mein Gott, what a little beauty,' said Biedermann. 'Where do you come from, Fräulein?'

'I remember you well, Herr Biedermann, and I have always admired you. I hope you will accept this cake, which my mother and I have made for you.'

'With pleasure, Fräulein,' said the gross creature, immensely flattered. The conversation centred round the girl's beauty after she had gone out. Biedermann in particular was lavish in his praise. Suddenly they heard an ominous ticking coming from the box. But they did not get out in time. The whole room was blown to pieces . . .

Hilde was beheaded three weeks later, calm and happy.

(February 27, 1935)

Patrick Gordon-Walker *was an undergraduate at Christ Church where he later taught. Labour MP for Smethwick and then Leyton, he rose to be Foreign Secretary in 1964. He died in 1980.*

Richard Crossman *obtained a First in Classical Greats at New College where he was made a fellow and taught political philosophy until 1937. He wrote poetry and became friends with W. H. Auden. Later he was leader of the Labour group on Oxford City Council, a cabinet minister and editor of the* New Statesman.

Frank Pakenham, *now* **Lord Longford,** *told the present writers of another magazine he started at the university,* The Oxford University Review. *'I wrote and asked Bernard Shaw, among others, for a message. I received the following reply: "Mr Shaw asks me to say that a magazine that stuffs its first number with messages no one wants to read, will fail and will deserve to. Even young Oxford should know better than that." Signed Blanche Patch, secretary.*

'I need hardly say that we made great play of it in the first number. Our posters carried the headline: "Message from Mr Bernard Shaw".'

Statements following Oswald Mosley's meeting in Oxford

P. Gordon-Walker, M.A. (Christ Church)

It is very difficult for the outsider who has not been to a Mosley meeting to realise the menace to democracy and free speech represented by his movement. It is not that the Fascists themselves go about directly causing violence and breaking up meetings; their technique is much more subtle and dangerous than that. This technique was well illustrated in the recent meeting in Oxford. From the very beginning a deliberate attempt was made to provoke the crowd and bring it to a high and excited pitch of indignation. The mere presence of Blackshirt stewards along the walls and round the platform was calculated to anger the crowd. There can be little doubt, I think, if Mosley spoke without those provocative, uniformed guards, that he would receive no more than normal heckling and that very soon the general feeling that he should be allowed at least to have a fair hearing would prevail. (It is interesting to note that Mr Crossman, who suggested to Mosley during the rough-house that, if he withdrew his Blackshirts, we on our part would guarantee him a fair hearing, was thrown roughly off the platform for his pains. After the Nazi Horst Wessel song had been several times played on the loudspeaker, Mosley suddenly appeared on the platform. His first words were that interrupters would be ejected 'courteously and quietly'. The greater part of his speech was designed to be provocative: he persisted in pretending that an audience, in which workers predominated, consisted only of young undergraduates; he taunted the leaders of the Labour Party with office-seeking and cowardice, etc., etc. The most provocative thing of all, however, was the steady advance, foot by foot, of a squad of twenty tough-looking Blackshirts, down the centre gangway from the back of the hall down towards the platform.

Mosley after a time had quite deliberately got the audience into a dangerous temper, when it was obvious that any spark would set them off. At this moment he suddenly ordered an interrupter, who was persistently asking some questions, to be ejected. It was no doubt the purest coincidence that the advancing phalanx in the centre gangway had just reached this man. Mosley's command was curious, after his announcement that interrupters would be courteously ejected: it was 'Chuck that man out.' I have never seen a man so brutally set upon. The phalanx of twenty surrounded the man; he was dragged off his chair by the face, one Blackshirt digging his nails into his cheek. At the same moment another body of Blackshirts dashed up from the platform, bringing the odds to about thirty to one. At this moment, had the man been courteously requested to go, nothing might have happened. The excessive brutality with which he was handled, however, set a spark to the crowd. It would have needed a man of iron control not to attempt to defend the man, who was being dragged along the floor, and being rabbit-punched from behind. He had been unable to make a move in his own defence. In thirty seconds the hall was in pandemonium, steel chairs were flying, fists were being used. Several people whom I know were only drawn in to defend the women and some young undergraduates who were being attacked four to one.

The appearance of a handful of police brought to an end an ugly situation in which someone might well have been killed. As regards the police, as far as I could observe, the ordinary constable was very fair and was prepared to take names of Blackshirts accused by the public of assault. A few higher officials seemed to me to have a very different attitude: they assumed the public in the wrong; one, at least, refused to take the name of a Blackshirt accused of assault. In contrast, the attitude of this official towards Mosley himself was courteous and even subservient.

It may be worth saying a word about Mosley's speech itself. He was extraordinarily disappointing as a speaker; I can think of a dozen in England who are far finer, simply as orators. Unlike Hitler, Mosley is totally unable to convey even the appearance of sincerity and faith. When Mosley attempted to unfold his constructive case, it was so dull that his audience became evidently bored, and even heckling came to an end. Mosley did not even reveal himself as able to deal well with hecklers; he easily allowed himself to be thrown off his stride, and the argument of his speech was constantly lost. So little did Mosley appear to think of the attractiveness of his own oratory that he constantly held it as a threatened punishment over the heads of his audience that he would continue for half an hour longer than he would otherwise have done. He made constant slips, unworthy of a practised speaker, which turned the laugh against himself, as when he said, speaking of Russia, 'I will not use Fascist or prejudiced figures.'

It is imperative that the public should realise how easily Mosley can break up free speech. Not himself breaking up meetings, but by deliberately provoking his audience and then causing a rough-house. If we are not careful, Mosley, acting in the name of order and free speech, will be able to destroy both in one town after another.

R. H. S. Crossman, M.A. (New College)

It was quite obvious from the opening words of his speech that Mosley relied not on argument but on provocation. The steady advance foot by foot for the first hour of a Blackshirt phalanx down the main gangway, the incessant jibes at the audience which was mainly working class for being silly undergraduates who had never done a stroke of work, could only have one result. When Mosley ordered a questioner to be flung out he must have known there would be a free fight. Although he had constantly promised that interruptors would be courteously removed, what actually happened was that at least twenty Blackshirts leapt upon one man and kicked and rabbit-punched him unmercifully. I cannot pretend I am sorry that an Oxford audience did not take this 'sitting down'.

Two things are worth remarking on. Firstly, the stupidity of the organisers of the meeting in putting steel chairs in the Carfax Assembly Rooms on a night when they must have known there would be trouble. Secondly, the ineffectiveness of the police. They must have known there would be danger of disturbance, but when the row started there were certainly not more than four or five policemen present and they were right at the back of the hall where they were unable to see what was going on. If Mosley ever speaks in Oxford again it should be made perfectly clear (1) that the stewards must be Oxford people, and (2) that the police, if they are present, should be present in sufficient numbers and should be scattered throughout the hall. It is Mosley's peculiar art to make decent law-abiding people see red. In that case it might be better for the decent law-abiding people to leave him to mouth in a vaccum.

Frank Pakenham, M.A. (Christ Church)

I warmly endorse Mr Crossman's comments. Whether or no Mosley and his agents are guilty of having committed criminal offences on Monday is for the courts to decide; but in any case no decent person who was present is likely to attend any more meetings addressed by this grotesque clown. For his dupes, even for the wretched quartet who continued to rabbit-punch me for some time after the uproar had subsided, I feel nothing but pity. They looked timid and uneasy, and anything but happy at having to carry out their leader's work. Thank God, Oxford is not likely to be impressed by the mechanical bleating of this gimcrack fencing master, so facetious about working-class accents, so deaf to the absurdity of his own.

(May 27, 1936)

Lindsay Anderson, *now a film director and critic, edited the cinema quarterly* Sequence *after leaving Wadham College. He wrote in 1952, 'I came across a batch of copies of* The Isis, *each one folded back so that it lay open at the film page. One look was enough. What callowness — what unsureness — what inability to manipulate language. They went very quickly into the dustbin.' When he heard of the anthology, he added, 'Criticism is really too difficult and responsible a business for the young and inexperienced, particularly as they are bound to adopt the arrogant attitudes nowaday fashionable in the media. However, to be reminded of one's juvenile attempts at smartness is salutary: it makes one forgive — or at least understand — more easily.*
'I'd like to revisit A Night in Paradise, *though.'*

At the Films

The Ritz: Anchors Aweigh
Another Musical for Metro-Goldwyn-Morons: in not unpleasing technicolor, with Gene Kelly, Frank Sinatra and Kathryn Grayson. Here is talent enough for an entertaining hour and a half, but *Anchors Aweigh* is no exception to the approved rule, and talent and colour is accordingly squandered on the routine two and a half hours of vulgarity and dreary

mutual deception. The leering innuendoes of the first hour or so are perhaps the most unpleasant part of the film; later things cheer up with two brilliant dance sequences and the appearance of a lively new personality in Pamela Britton. But every time the film threatens to become enjoyable, up pops José Iturbi to rattle off the Donkey Serenade with his right hand while conducting a full symphony orchestra with his left, or to lead an ensemble of twenty teen-age grand-pianists in a performance of Liszt's second Hungarian Rhapsody in the Hollywood Bowl. Mr Iturbi—this is a definite judgment—is now the smuggest thing on celluloid, and almost the most vulgar.

Kathryn Grayson you may remember as a charming, pleasantly unaffected young singer; stardom has ironed most of that out of her and hidden what is left under an impenetrable mask of paint. Frank Sinatra cannot act but has a pleasing personality and does as well as he can with his songs; Gene Kelly's dancing is a delight, and the only thing (besides my conscience) that kept me at my post to the end.

(*May 1, 1946*)

Electra: A Night in Paradise
It all depends, I suppose, what you mean by Paradise . . . This particular paradise is technicolored, lavatorial in architecture, sub-adolescent in general conception and peopled by hard but shapely chorus girls, a cluster of ham actors, Turban Bey and Merle Oberon (ageing but still game). The plot concerns, as far as I could make out, Croesus, Aesop, and the Delphi racket. For the first few, incredible minutes it is all quite entertaining (Merle's greeting to Aesop Bey, for instance—'Not *the* Aesop, of Aesop's Fables!'), but such amusement soon gives place to impatience and impatience to the final horror—prolonged, unmitigated boredom. Still, one man's Hell . . .

(*October 16, 1946*)

83

Kenneth (Peacock) Tynan *was writing theatre criticism even before he came up to Oxford. A flamboyant figure, he directed Peter Parker in a university production of* Hamlet. *Tony Richardson said of Tynan's talents after his death in 1980, 'It was a different kind of criticism, because it was so visual and so precise. I mean, his descriptions of acting and performance had a sort of gusto which was very unlike anything that was being written at the time. He was able photographically and wittily to describe what an actor or a performer did, which no one else had the gift for.'*

Opéra Bouffe à la D'Oyly Carte

New Theatre: The Gondoliers
Sing Ho! and tra-la-la! for the D'Oyly Carte is amongst us for a brief season of Tum-tiddy-tum. And what exuberant, bedizened dears they are! There may be unlovely caperings and luckless guesses at tone and pitch, but for the most part this neatly dressed and thickly painted company is as spry in foot and voice as a comparable society of well-preserved, middle-aged seals. They toss Gilbert's beckoning and responding phrases one to another with trained, circus agility. Should they drop or fumble one, it is no matter; the situation can be saved by a frozen flash of teeth and Sheridan's traditional 'glance at

the pit'. They rarely stop smiling: the men smile brazenly, the women coyly. It is all very amiable, and very well-drilled. It is also very bogus, varying between Victorian parlour-whimsey at its best and Vesta-Victorian pantomime at its worst. If you can imagine M. Maurice Chevalier in Meilhac and Halévy, you have some notion of its continental counterpart, as well as of something about three times as entertaining.

What these hard-toiling players need is a little *pizzicato* of the spirit. There is an abundance of it in the music; and it cries out for the light, kindling touch of the aristocrat. Gilbert demands, above all, poise and genuine refinement of temper and diction, not bored, exaggerated mock-heroics, or the utterance of every long word with grotesque contortions of the lips expressive of vulgar, astonished contempt. Aristocracy of mind, of mind sportive and zestful, is the first requisite for a singer of Gilbert and Sullivan. There were people singing on Monday night (and being applauded to the echo for it) whose voices were less suited to D'Oyly Carte than to the sale of Doyly Pipers.

The Gondoliers is a pleasing tale of foundlings and mistaken identity, of rags and riches. Deprive it of grace and lightness, and its intrinsic absurdity drags it to the ground. It was sung by a number of plump gentlemen and a much larger number of plump ladies: most of them, unhappily, of determinate age. It may seem uncharitable to disparage physique and years; but in this kind of entertainment there must be comeliness and gingerness in the women, and freshness and charm in the men. The words and music are sprucely juggled together; let them be sprucely performed. Oscar Wilde once said that it was tragic to see how many young men started life with perfect profiles and ended by entering some useful profession. May I publicly exhort such young men to think twice, and then plunge in to save the D'Oyly Carte? They are sadly lacked.

It would be unfair to say much of the individual performances. Mr C. William Morgan, under-studying for Mr Graham Clifford, transformed the Duke of Plaza-Toro completely and unforgivably into Baron Stonybroke of Hardup Hall, in which establishment the gentlemen playing the two Gondoliers would have made admirable Broker's Men. Mr Richard Walker, who is George Robey's shell, played the

Grand Inquisitor with a kind of leering tolerance which must have made Torquemada turn in his grave at several hundred revs a minute. Miss Margaret Mitchell, the Queen of Baratria, was pretty, and let it go at that. She played the Queen all evening as though under constant fear that someone might play the King. Fortunately, Mr Herbert Garry never began to. Miss Ella Halman has a flawless plum-velvet voice, and was a delight. There were some other principal players, but they had names like Vendetta and Ravioli, which is very confusing.

Once, at a concert of string quartets, a friend whispered to Bernard Shaw: 'These men have been playing together for twenty years.' 'Surely,' said Shaw, 'we can't have been here that long?' I react in like manner to the D'Oyly Carte. But do go to the New Theatre; Gilbert's lyrics are brilliantly contrived, and you can buy the 'Book of Words' inside the theatre for 1/6d. And then you will have the rest of the evening free.

(May 23, 1946)

Ludovic Kennedy, *later a genial television journalist and author, liked to pretend to be a hermit at Oxford, according to an* Isis *'Idol': 'But do hermits really play the drums in nightclubs; do they join the navy in wartime; do they write best-sellers like* Sub-Lieutenant; *do they form clubs like the Oxford University Writers Club; are they to be found in select drawing-rooms discussing the future of the novel with Charles Morgan; and do they wander about the more remote Scottish islands with a romantic look in their eyes?' Yet he still found time to edit* The Isis.

Jehovah Was a Witness

Green envy will creep into the hearts of housewives when they learn that until recently I had never entered a Food Office. But for seven years I was a sailor, and naval victuals are, so to speak, taxed at source. At the University, where I am now, they ask you for your ration-book and the responsibility of keeping you alive is then theirs.

They asked me for mine the other day. But could I lay hands on it? No! Had my scout seen it? No! Had Harris, who lives upstairs, borrowed it? No! Then you must go to the Food Office and get another one.

I went to the Food Office between lectures, and was shown into a room that resembled a small post office. Along three sides ran a wooden counter supporting an iron grille, and behind the grille, spaced out like seed potatoes in the spring, sat seven ladies. A poster in front of each proclaimed her business.

The lady to whom I was directed was quite versatile. In addition to Lost Ration-Books, she specialized in Old Age Tea and Applications for Slaughtering Pigs. Note *slaughtering*! Not killing, mark you, or even Putting Pigs to Sleep: to end the life of a pig, one must *slaughter* it. I shuddered.

'Good morning,' she said briskly, 'and what can I do for *you*?'

I restrained from inquiring whether I looked senile enough to require Old Age Tea, or by what stretch of imagination she could conceive me slaughtering pigs.

'I've lost,' I said, 'my ration-book.'

'Ah ha!' she exclaimed as though glad of it, 'you want Form R.G.5.A.' She rummaged among a pile of papers and whipped out a sheet. 'Fill this up, and bring it back here. Pen and ink over there.'

The completing of Form R.G.5.A. did not take long. Most of the questions concerned how, when and where the ration-book was lost, and the answer 'I wish I knew' seemed adequate for all. I took the form back to the counter.

'Very good,' said the lady, giving it a cursory glance, 'now you must get it witnessed.'

'Witnessed?'

'There's a list of responsible persons on the back. Then bring it back here.'

I turned the form over and studied the list of responsible persons. They gave you a liberal choice. You could have a Doctor, or a Minister of Religion, or a Police Officer Not Below The Rank Of Sergeant; a Clerk of a Trade Union would do, and so would a School Teacher, a Captain in the Salvation Army, and a Warden of a Residential Establishment.

Outside in the street, I saw that I had a quarter of an hour before my lecture. Could I find a witness in time?

Several people were passing along the pavement. Was this tall military figure clutching a bag of Brussels sprouts the Warden of a Residential Establishment? Could that mild creature in the dirty mackintosh be a Salvation Army Captain in mufti? How did one recognize a Clerk of a Trade Union? There was a policeman directing traffic at the crossroads, but he was only a private.

At ten to eleven I gave it up, and headed for my lecture. I had hardly turned the corner when who should come bearing down on me but a Minister of Religion. I seized his arm joyfully, and pushing Form R.G.5.A. into his hand, explained my purpose.

'I suppose it's all right,' he said, eyeing me suspiciously.

'Quite,' I assured him. 'If you'll just sign here and put your address. You are a resident, aren't you?'

'Yes,' he said, 'I'm a don at Jesus.'

He pulled out a pen and scribbled along the bottom of the form. I muttered my thanks, pocketed the form, and hurried back to the Food Office. With luck I should arrive for my lecture on time, the owner of a new ration-book.

'Here we are,' I said heartily, sweeping up to the counter. 'Signed, sealed and delivered.'

The lady took the form and studied it keenly. Suddenly she looked up. Something told me that all was not well.

'I suppose,' she said acidly, 'you think that's funny!'

Even now, I can't make up my mind whether it was a perverted sense of humour or sheer nerves that made that parson do what he did. Against 'Signature of Witness' he had written 'Jesus'; against 'Address' the ink had run and the writing was illegible.

I missed my lecture of course, and when I got back to my rooms, there was an envelope with my scout's hand-writing. 'Sir,' it said, 'enclosed is ration-book found in your cake-tin.'

Next time I go to the Food Office, I shall apply to slaughter—yes *slaughter*, a pig. It will be more satisfying.

(*November 5, 1947*)

Alan Brien, *who has been since 1976 a film critic of the* Sunday Times, *went to Jesus College after serving as an air-gunner in the RAF during the war. He edited* The Isis.

In Defence of Oxford

Last term the *News Chronicle*, the Nanny of the Middle Classes, smoothed her dress, adjusted her pince-nez and editorially deplored our apathy. Dr Joad, after delivering his annual unchanging man-to-man chat to Oxford, occupied several columns of the *New Statesman* in explaining why we were apathetic, uncultivated and lacking in that rich charm which Oxford had bestowed upon him. If we allow these patronising homilies to pass unanswered we will deserve everything we get. In this article I originally intended to give only a passing kick at these moth-eaten Aunt Sallys, which have been set up by every writer since Antony à Wood who wished to make sensational copy out of Oxford, without singling out individuals. But this resolution was broken when I discovered in *Vogue*, all among the glossy ladies in the New Look, Ken Tynan letting his hair down to the New Length on the subject of Oxford.

Attacks on Oxford always come in two patterns; the Editorial, or prefabricated platitude, and the Individual, or Alma Pater, styles. Mr Tynan, with his combination of the incongruous adjective and the unusual noun, of the blue joke and the purple patch, the Wardour Street English and the New Yorker slang, specializes in the latter.

Mr Tynan in a tone of condescending sweetness, like Beverley Nichols and whipped cream, tells *Vogue* readers that although three-quarters of the undergraduates are ex-Service-men who talk of Tel-Aviv and nationalization and work hard, the people who matter are a few 'sensitive souls who live with a flair for abandon' and who form 'an aristocracy on Hellenic lines'. Now these fragile beings are recognized by the wearing of a 'golden satin shirt and a floppy velvet tie'. In other words, they are Mr Tynan and his reflections. This gay sensitive set are described as 'diffuse, macabre, irrational, effeminate—yes effeminate'. (The emphasis will be Mr Tynan's to the grave.) What are the high spots of this wonderful 'life of *snobbisme*' which makes it so superior to the poky hole-and-corner life that the rest of us lead? Apparently the holding of 'Nursery Parties' where all the guests come in gym-smocks and short pants and all feel, and admit to feeling, 'a need for maternal solace'! When not providing material in this way for Freudian case-histories, they spend their time measuring each other's brows over coffee and throwing exclusive parties on moon-lit barges. It seems impossible that Mr Tynan is not exercising his talent for malicious parody so reminiscent in his gossip-column chatter to Cyril Connolly's brilliant mock autobiography of a rather tarnished young thing, 'Where Engels Fears to Tread'. Here is a gobbet or two of Connolly:

'Parties! "Are you going to de Claverings tonight?" and woe betide the wretch who had to say no. Nothing much happened at the time but he soon felt he was on an ice-floe, drifting farther and farther away from land . . . De Claverings tonight! The candles burn in their sconces. The incense glows. Yquem and Avocado pears—a simple meal—but lots of both—with whisky for the hearties and champagne for the dons. And then dancing, while the canons go home over the quad.' This is the very accent of Tynan's article. Connolly goes on to anticipate the future. 'My twenty-firster! Fifty people in fancy dress. The orchestra from the Grand Ecart. As the college barge, which I had taken for the occasion, glided up the Cher., life's goblet seemed full to brimming.' I cannot resist just one quotation in which Connolly's hero, Christian de Clavering, forestalls Mr Tynan even in the matter of parties. 'I remember my tropical party when the punkah was heard for the first time in Egerton Crescent. Palms and bananas decorated the rooms. Some stewards from the P. & O. distributed Riestafel and planter's punch. The guests wore shorts, sarongs or nothing at all.' To have one's style and outlook parodied so deftly years *before* one has adopted them, this is the most bitter of ignominies for a writer. Still, a man who claims to live in 'an orchidaceous hothouse' should be more careful about pulling down the blinds.

I have concentrated on Mr Tynan because he is not only the most able of Oxford's denigrators but also the most courageous. Few of the others dare to exhibit their own tastes and behaviour as the only correct standard and none have dared to dismiss most of their contemporaries as unworthy of consideration. Oxford, concludes Tynan, consists to all intents of the one twentieth of those who 'live with a flair for abandon,' and the one twentieth of 'good sycophants who relax and admire them' while the remaining nine-tenths, that is the rest of us, are 'dumb and oaf-like.'

This is as absurd as it would be for, say, the Railway Society to denounce as tasteless philistines those of us who can just distinguish the Scotsman from the Rocket. But the important thing is that we should refute this publicly. Oxford, thank God, is a city of cliques and its greatest charm is that no matter how eccentric your personality, how bizarre your dress and eclectic your interests, you can find sympathetic companions. (Mr Tynan is an excellent example of this.) We all have our personal recipe for the full life. Sydney Smith said that his idea of Heaven was eating *foie gras* to the sound of trumpets; my idea of Hell is eating Grade 3 salmon to the sound of Union speeches. One man prefers to spend his evenings on those Elizabethan prodigies of tedium, George Turberville and Barnabe Googe, while another will rather attend a lantern slide lecture at the Synoptic Palimpsest Club. But few of us have the arrogance to dismiss anyone who does not fit our personal pattern. Even so unique a person as Mr Tynan has a place in our scheme of things—every society has its buffoon. And as Hazlitt said of Gifford, the Editor of *The Quarterly*, 'He is admirably fitted for this position by a happy combination of defects, natural and acquired, and in the event of his retirement, it will be difficult to provide him with a suitable successor.'

(May 5, 1948)

Derek Cooper *is today a broadcaster with the BBC and has a regular food column in* The Observer. *Graham Greene sent a telegram congratulating him on his* Isis *piece, 'This is Hell'.*

When the Lights Go Up

The growth of the film-going habit in the last thirty years has been accompanied by the gradual emergence of a new set of characters. We see them only when the lights come up, but are intimately aware of their presence without needing our eyes to confirm what our other senses have only surmised. They are in direct line of descent from the Chaucerian pilgrim, the Hogarthian tipler or Dickensian drab. The tight-lipped and impassive, those who remain unmoved through food-flash and death-by-fire, add nothing to the atmosphere of the cinema but their own carbon dioxide. The possibilities of mass-incarceration in the dark lie beyond their imagination, and it is not to them that this piece is dedicated. Hats off then to the Active Lovers, the Chronic Asthmatics, the Weak-Bladdered, the Libido-Releasers, the Claustrophobics, and the Children in Arms. But hats off first to:

The Inveterate Eaters, who never eat unhygienically. All their food, from rollmops to sticks of nougat, is embalmed in layers of paper which require to be unpeeled with cautious and dilatory movements. Once unravelled, the cream bun or nutty-trifle may roll off your neighbour's knees and on to the floor. If you are wise you will squash it and apologise. This forestalls diving operations. If you are not ruthless in the destruction of fallen food, sticky hands will soon embrace your leg and claw the ground from under your shoes. With a morsel in their mouths the Inveterate Eaters are transformed. Peristalsis begins. The nutcracker teeth clack rhythmically, the glottis quivers with activity, and even the cheeks assist, for they act as a sounding-board to the frenzy of digestion. Later, when you retire to bed, you will be able to recollect in tranquillity the virtues of the Eater for his tangerine pips are sown in your turn-ups and his toffee-papers cling affectionately to your overcoat, sticky testimonials of your ordeal. An even more vivid figure is:

The Flamethrower, who in his direst form affects a pipe which he handles with the ineptitude of the novice. Every few minutes an Etna of flame is flinted into being and amid much sucking and blowing (how musical is the passage of dottle through a pipe-stem) the trusty old briar, newly varnished with creosote and brimstone, belches into renewed life. Like a true phoenix, it literally arises from the ashes of its former self. You share his favourite tobacco by proxy and with tearducts sluicing peer humidly through the smoke screen eddying from his portable bonfire. On your left there may be another Flamethrower. If he is smoking a cigarette it will be held in the hand nearest your eye and the elbow of that hand will be perching steadily on the arm-rest (your arm-rest, from which ever end of the row you look at it). Whether it's pipe, cigarette, or cigar, keep an eye skinned for sparks and a nostril alert for the inimitable odour of burning clothes. They're bound to be yours. Under such circumstances you might easily become a:

One Man Fan. This colourful character is convinced that the cooling system of the cinema has broken down (in off-the-circuit cinemas he *is* the cooling system) and that only the agitated flapping of a magazine will save the entire audience from asphyxiation. In his sublimest moments the One Man Fan displays paranoiac symptoms. He convinces himself that there's a plot afoot to kill him, and that the soft-footed usherettes have wittingly clamped down on the air supply. His only escape from a diabolically planned piece of unjustifiable homicide is to lash the few molecules of oxygen remaining, into a maelstrom. The Human Fans never go down without fighting. Jollier, and much more ubiquitous are:

The Technicians, a brotherhood composed of amateur hobbledehoys who 'know how it's done'. Authoritative in sideburns and handpainted ties, they intersperse their gumchewing with inside information. You are several thousand miles away on Bikini atoll, eyes feasting on the gyrations of a bevy of grass-skirted orchids, when a voice rasps in your ear: 'Synchronised double-exposed back-projection—a bit of old footage from *Pacific Paradise*, a dash of eccentric 3mm multifocals, and Bob's your uncle . . . you gotta hand it to 'em though, it's a sooper dooper effect.' It was. Feeling like a Maskelyne who had been publicly foxed by Find the Lady, you sink into your tip-up. Another voice you will come to love, belongs to:

The Connoisseur, who is to be found in draughty halls off the Edgware Road seeing *Mother* for the ninth time: '*Exquisite* montage . . . My God, Lola, it's tearing my heart out . . . this can't go on.' At a film of his own choice he is noisy enough but just listen to him when he gets mixed up in the B-feature that helps to pay for the foreign film: 'Oh, yes . . . here it comes— double-take when he throws the custard pie . . . For Pete's sake, not that bloody flag *again* . . . standby for celestial choir—*with* Nova-chord.' His eyes are always on the run looking for tricky angles and rhythmic cutting and his laugh comes a split second before the sub-title—but you have to be quick. You will be unfortunate if you find the Connoisseur in the same row as:

The Kind Friend, who is usually accompanied by Auntie— an Auntie bereft of sight, hearing and reason. Is that curvy lady on the screen really a Bryn Mawr psychiatrist or is she just a two-bit interne masquerading as a zombie? And from behind you hear: 'Oo-er! Look out! He's creeping up on you,' a stifled scream, 'He's drawn a gun—no, it's a knife . . . you sure you can see, Rhoda?' 'Yersss!' 'That's Dana Truff, the new starlet. He was in *Picturelover* last week. You see, that tall one with the dimples is the father of the beauty-contest baby and he's lost all his money on the fruit machines . . . Ah, in'it luvverly . . . Rhoda, wake up!' The Kind Friend insists on seeing the programme round twice so you are no more able to escape from her than from:

Flash Harry, the organist. He caters for the Hummers and the Whistlers and his repertoire is grotesquely catholic. Bach and Balfe, Tchaikovsky and Tobani are attacked with a misplaced gusto which drags in the whole gamut of experience from sleigh bells to train whistles. The wurlitzer vibrates, blushes in all the shades of neon known to its makers and a mighty vortex of sound roars out of the walls. Flash Harry rides his machine with the savoir vivre of a musician, if not the talent. While he pummels the keys, hands and feet caressing his unlovely mistress, a succession of lurid slides pop on to the screen—bearing in child's writing the words you are to utter. While this grisly bag of tricks is being worked the audience are devout at the shrine of music. Their communal discord rises like cheap incense to the roof and the sweet-papers rustle autumnally. Flash Harry is the most popular of men, much in demand on:

Amateur Nights. If you disapprove of amateur nights avoid cinemas with Sistine chapel roofs and Louis-Quatorze stairways, prelude to disappointment. Amateur nights flourish in the super cinemas (ACROPOLIS—please pronounce it UH-*Krop*-ERLISS). If you have a genial soul and a big hand you will be able to deal with the situation with your usual tact. *Trees* on the electric saw will leave you as unmoved as *Ave Maria* on the bones. And next time the lights go up . . . just watch your step.

(February 23, 1949)

This Is Hell – Nor Am I Out of It

Meeting a refugee from Greene-land

He leant against the hoarding by the picture palace and felt the dull heavy pain rising in the pit of his stomach. The tablet which he placed on the tip of his tongue lay flat and tasteless like a communion wafer until he crunched it into a powder and swallowed. His sharp, injured gaze followed the shopgirls and their boyfriends as they hurried giggling and jostling into the vulgar foyer of the cinema. Each time the swing door opened it released a draught of dry, hygienic air and he wished he was inside. Coughing, he drew the thin mac about his shoulders and a vicious gust of wind set the refuse and papers swirling down the street. It began to rain heavily.

I went over and introduced myself. We disappeared into a pub. 'It was cold out there,' he said, 'Just waiting . . . for nothing. Expecting . . . nothing. And always the shabby lovers arm in arm; the long waking hours; and the phone that never rings. The tasteless food and the half-remembered sin—what'll you have?' But I was already coming back from the bar. We sat down and I asked him what it felt like to be a Graham Greene character. He coloured at my question and took a quick sip of his mild. The noise and chatter of the bar insulated us from the fictional world.

'How did you guess?' and the dirty fingernails went up nervously to pluck at the frayed Lancing tie. I told him and he blushed again. I asked him what the plot was; what was his name? He smiled, and wiped his forehead with a grubby handkerchief. 'I don't know really. Maybe a chase . . . adrift in a world of hate and betrayal—travelling under a dozen aliases, but always the same seedy rotter.' He examined his clothes disgustedly: 'Same shabby shoes, the badly-darned socks, and the suit that's too old to crease. The middle-aged wreck drenched in sin. I could tell you the background without thinking. The mortgaged villa with the peeling walls. Perpetual worry over the job that's never quite worth the effort—the ailing wife and the horror of growing old. It gives you the pip,' he said, 'But I expect it's all got literary merit. Now I'd like to be one of Mr Waugh's characters. Toney surroundings, mixing with the upper crust, no troubles, and everybody eating out of your hand—and it always works out tidily in the end.'

I suggested that we should go through his pockets and find out what he was really supposed to be. The first thing we saw was a final demand note for the rates. It was addressed to Fred Rennitt: 'In debt already, before the party begins,' he complained, 'It gives me the pip. We're finished before we start.' He pulled out a child's whistle, a bakelite crucifix, a toffee, and a doctor's prescription—he had an ulcer alright. But Rennitt wasn't looking at any of these. He'd found a wallet and was busy poring over some faded snaps. The young-old face that stared up so confidently from the yellowing cricket group was a juvenile Rennitt. 'Captain of the 1st XI, by the looks of it,' and imperceptibly he squared his shoulders. The down and out Old Boy reassured and strengthened.

'The innocence of childhood and the first confession . . . the pain of adolescence and the discovery of evil. And then—no more signposts, no love, no values any more; only the immense horror of sin and the belief in absolution . . .' I plucked at his sleeve and reminded him that he wasn't on duty yet. It wasn't easy to break the habit, he said. 'I've been through a lot of these books you know, and that way of thinking gets a grip on you. You really become fascinated with ageing tarts and unfrocked clergymen.'

We looked a bit more and found that Rennitt was a commercial traveller. 'Agent' was the word he settled for. There was a badly developed photo of a scraggy working-class woman dandling a rickety baby on her knee. That discovery didn't please Rennitt; neither did the St Anthony medal with his name on it. 'You mark my words—I'll end up bad.' His lonely eyes began to explore the pub and I saw him savour the fly-blown ceiling and the slatternly women in their cheap clothes. Outside the kids were playing in the gutter and a blind man tapped unheeded down the street. Rennitt turned on me furiously. 'My God, look at them . . . they're all horrible, seedy, vulgar; but none of them beyond redemption.' He threw back his head and laughed, 'Oh, I've been here before alright. The false bonhomie and the smutty joke—the love that's nothing but soured lust!' He pointed to the piano with a trembling hand. A large, jolly woman, her breasts quaking with mirth, was beating time to the music with an empty glass. The words of a bawdy song fell from her lips. 'That's Ida,' I said, 'I don't think she would have liked you.' She screamed with laughter and the glasses rang behind the bar. I told him I'd read this story, but he wasn't in it. I explained about Pinkie and Rose, and the razor gangs, but he wasn't interested any more.

'What does one do?', he asked, and I didn't know how to

answer him. 'Why not try Africa,' I suggested. He asked me if it was corrupt and shabby there and I had to admit that it was. Rennitt paled and moistened his lips: 'There'll be a war, I suppose.' But already he was exploring the future—the tin roofs under the tropical sky and the conflict of love and duty, good and evil fighting in the equatorial heat. He took up the old trilby and the greasy mac and walked towards the door.

(April 27, 1949)

William Rees-Mogg, *future editor of* The Times, *won a scholarship to Balliol at the age of seventeen, but the Second World War intervened and he returned to the university after serving in the RAF. An* Isis *'Idol' noted in 1951 that Rees-Mogg liked to listen to 'Housewives' Choice' and had an ambition to be Chancellor of the Duchy of Lancaster. 'By lunchtime,' it continued, 'he wanders slowly towards the Carlton, dressed in a suit of indeterminate age, shape and colour.' His 'one vice' was occasional journalism.*

Free Speech Comes Second!

People are always talking about free speech. It is a tiresome habit. As a slogan it has the advantage of ambiguity: for this reason politicans talk about it. Politicians, who think many odd things, appear to believe that free speech is a public institution cherished by the public, but free speech, to a politician, means his right to tell lies, or the truth, about his opponent and his opponent's right to tell the truth, or lies, about him. To all sane men, and the public, unlike politicians, is sane, this process is boring and childish. Government by discussion degenerates into government by abuse. It is certainly not what ordinary people mean by free speech: it is certainly not a freedom which ordinary people die to defend.

Recently the problems of free speech have been unusually

noticeable. The *Sunday Times* want to see a book withdrawn. They say on the front page that is not the sort of book to be left lying around where women might pick it up. The law of libel is being tinkered with by a Commission, which has now reported. On the Gold Coast the Colonial Secretary confiscates books by Mr Creech Jones, and local papers retract statements they have printed under duress by the local administration. In Malta some newspaper or other is in very hot water. In Russia musicians, scientists and economists kneel on the penitent's stool to recant their error. Mr Bolam is still serving his three months in our own country. All these things happen at much the same time. We may ask what it is all about, and whether what is happening ought to be happening.

It is always simple, and sometimes intellectually pleasing, to draw distinctions. In the present matter they are rather obvious and may even be helpful. There are two forms of free speech which may be objected to. Some people are worried by moral problems: they dislike hearing naughty words. Some people are worried by political problems: they are always looking for a bomb under the bed. I, myself, am in the second category and shall thus consider the question of political censorship first. Censorship is an ugly word: it does not follow that censors are ugly people. It is possible to establish a censorship in two ways. One can set up a board of censors who read everything they find published, and spend the rest of their time listening to possibly censorable speeches; or one can establish a standard, impose it by law and hit people on the head who go against it. This is less trouble to all concerned. It is also what now happens.

It is inevitable that some political censorship should exist. If people are allowed to say or write: 'Let us shoot the Cabinet!' they will find other people to agree with them. Indeed the advice may be good advice: the Cabinet may be a bad Cabinet. For the sake of public order we refuse to allow people to publish such advice, and prefer bad Cabinets to dead ones. We do not allow a man to shoot people; we do not even allow him to recommend that people should be shot; are we right to stop him advocating the establishment of a Government that will shoot people whom we think ought to be left unshot? We know that Fascist and Communist Governments have the

102

habit of removing people they do not like. Should we therefore allow Fascists and Communists to support unhindered a cause which will lead, if successful, to people being removed? If we are idiots or Liberals we shall say that free speech is more important than human life. If we are sane men we shall say that those parties should be censored unless it is more convenient to us to let them be.

Some people ask me 'Quis custodiet?' A democratically elected Government (sweet phrase to gull the simple minded, in this case meaningful) has every right to censor those who want to destroy the constitution. The people we choose to govern us have a right to stop other people persuading us to let them kill us. Every attempt is made by well-meaning people to obscure this simple truth. That is because the well-meaning and the clear-headed are not always together. No Government has a right to stop criticism. No Government has a right to ban any party which is a democratic party in our sense, but every Government has a duty to protect its citizens from false friends, from parties who respect the gun but not the ballot box. Political censorship is therefore justifiable when it is required to secure the basic liberty and even the existence of the State.

The great danger of any censorship is that it spreads. If there is to be an extended political censorship in this country, as, of course, there soon will be, will have to be, it must be carefully watched. There will, I think, always be plenty of people to watch it. The danger of moral censorship is that fat-heads are always urging it on, and that it is too seldom effectively opposed. Morality in England is almost always sexual morality. Therefore, as I hate to break conventions, in considering moral censorship I really consider only censorship of sexually inflammatory works. Indeed these, and the more obvious of these, are the only ones ever censored. The subtler perversions of sadism riot in our cheap literature freely, while one honest word to describe a dishonest action arouses the Puritans in their thousands. It is probably necessary to point out once again how stupid our laws against obscene publication are. Any policeman is thought a judge of decency. Rabelais has been banned and the Old Testament certainly could be. The effect of our law is obvious. Bad, filthy, nasty trash is safe.

Novels are published weekly which snigger and suggest, but any serious attempt to write a serious book frankly is greeted with abuse. The trouble is that our common informers, our staid editors, know very little about pornography. They do not read the books that do the harm: they feel hurt by important books that tell the truth.

What is the conclusion? That we shall have to muzzle the assassin parties, which will mean more political censorship. That we should have a reformed censorship of indecency, conducted by experts, that is to say that we should employ experts in pornography to tell us what books are cheaply suggestive and what books are not. That of course will annoy the Puritans; it will stop their fun.

(May 11, 1949)

Shirley Catlin *(now better known as Shirley Williams) was at Somerville College. In an* Isis *piece written to accompany Robert Robinson's article about the drama society tour of America in which she starred alongside Peter Parker, she wrote, 'America is Janus-faced and yet simple, passionate, single-minded and bursting with confidence. She demands to be fallen in love with at first sight.'*

One Woman's Week

Eights Week is that lull in the storm when people stop being Oxford in order to show off Oxford. In these butterfly-winged days Oxford recalls the minuets of its past in the sambas of its present. The hotels are crowded with imported girls, and relatives thirsting for a nip of their vanished youths. This is as much a mood as an occasion; the pride of exhibition, without exhibitionism.

The philosophers have given up Wittgenstein, wandering sheepishly down the towpaths; poets and journalists have cut their hair off, or at least lost their expressions of cultivated dissipation; even the socialites have dropped the sparkless wit of the last twenty cocktail parties in favour of a monologue on the visitors. Everyone relaxes into sun and sandwiches, and those who never relax strive hard at gracious living.

But Eights Week suffers from many different interpretations. I remember a habit of American schools that I used to resent intensely, the Parent-Teacher Conference. Psychologically I expect it was sound, but it felt too much like the powers that were ganging up against you. There is always that element in Eights Week, too. All your relatives arrive, hawk-eyed on the platform, hunting memories of their pasts or truths of your present. The shades of the school hat settle down again on a slightly lined forehead. Hellos are carefully purged of all meaning. (*Who was that? Oh, just a friend . . .*) The colleges become museum pieces or boarding schools (*What was that? A bump . . .*), except on the river, where they are just colours. There is the effort to try to remember whose oars are green-tipped (*What's a bump?*) and who won last year (*Yes, but I don't see how it works*), to notice in an undertone who is where with who, and whether you ought to wave or not. Then the infuriating habit parents have of telling you how many hours you ought to sleep when they should realise that your relationship with this particular audience of acquaintances is based on a sophistication as tinkling and polished as an eighteenth-century chandelier. The nearer you are to your childhood the more you want to forget it, to bury it for ever in cigarettes, whisky and wild, wild women.

There are also the other women, appearing in trainloads and cartwheel hats. For a week they are in power, delicately possessive, delightfully correct. We who trail about toasting crumpets, tidying rooms, unravelling rooms, discovering the man if we can in every gentleman, we are sacrificed to pride and prejudice. Eights Week is hardly a ripple on the surface beyond St Giles' and Magdalen Bridge.

The Eights Week Ball is the plum in the pudding, depending upon the festival atmosphere. The quad is star-studded with daisies and paste-pots, the strawberries are morsels of ambrosia in the melting ice-cream, and the tails from Folly Bridge are the acme of sartorial elegance. Perhaps you can forget the red-faced band and remember with Rumi that he who dwells in the dance dwells in God. Particularly in a primaeval tango. But the daze can be broken with little blasts of criticism. I remember a dance I once went to in which I spent two hours while the insipid dawn was washing out everyone's faces arguing about the pronunciation of the word orgy. By the end of the argument a graceful compliment was lost in hundreds of razor-edged words. The opportunity to discover the meaning, too, was irretrievably gone. I later lost him for ever in a top room and a bottle of Benedictine. Preserve your mind in any liquid you like, but let it alone in Eights Week.

But Eights Week is no time for carping or crusades. The world purrs in the sun and the gargoyles split their stone faces in smiles. The bitch goddess Success is thrown in the river like Zuleika, and she will only be rescued by good Trinity men. With Novalis and the fairies we must agree, the more poetic the more true. There are imps in the buttercups and Naiads in the river beyond the Parks. The moon stares at her pale face and hollow eyes in the water, and the bells clang out the empty hours. So why bother to think when there is nothing to think about? The only reality in this humming week is the appearance of things, the opium of summer in the air.

(May 17, 1950)

Robert Robinson's *article on America was reprinted in* Time *magazine a few weeks later and caused a storm. One angry American wrote, 'I gather that Robinson's satiric weapon is a bludgeon rather than the rapier, the broadsword rather than the scimitar. To his credit he reflects a certain rustic bluntness and stupid honesty.' Robinson edited* The Isis *in 1950, an 'Idol' commenting, 'He has a sharp, leaping wit which he can transfer into words without any trouble at all and his outlook on life is, at least superficially, tinged with cynicism.' It added, 'His* Isis *was frankly created for the popular taste, his editorials for his own.' On hearing of this reprinting of the women's debating society piece, he wrote, 'It might irritate more now than it did then—though that was considerable.'*

Hygienic Barbary

By night, then, we came to Hygienic Barbary, bewildered among the metal forests, the slot-machine reserves, wide-eyed along the untrodden ways dedicated to the auto; laved our tripes in coca-cola, ate light fawn lunches at 7/6 a go, saw Jackson and were unable to shake his hand for it was a great city, slept in our ladies' arms at many miles an hour, and rather suspected that Harrisburg would turn out to be a wire-haired terrier.

And that will be enough of Isisese which begins to give me a pain in the neck: I won't need a Thesaurus to describe America.

This aeroplane we went in was of sound but undecorative construction, with three propellors that went round when the driver pressed the starter, and a fourth that was induced to revolve by the homely but effective expedient of running the machine round the tarmac a couple of times against the wind. This put us all at our ease, and we were soon puking good-humouredly into the receptacles provided. Since it was as dark as hell for most of the 28 hours we were in the air, I am relieved of the responsibility of describing what the ground looked like from twenty-thousand feet. We floated into Idlewild Airport, NY on a tide of heat whose texture could almost be fingered: it was nighmarishly hot as we walked across a steaming tarmac that was like nothing so much as an asphalt playground thoughtfully provided by the Municipal Authority of Hell. A barren customs-and-immigration office with plastic floors and mercury-lighting smelt like a swimming-bath or an asylum ante-room, full of either swimmers or madmen, strangely selected: mitteleuropean commercial travellers with excited wives, and spiv-priests in Portobello Road jackets, their pockets bulging with phoney encyclicals—all queuing for the insulin-shock chamber.

After six hours they let us go, and we finally achieved inertia at 4 a.m. at Valparaiso (Ind.).

Now I want to talk about America, and if you don't think generalisations worth making at any time (and the critics, who know better than you, will support you), you'd better stop reading. Here then are some unequivocal judgments unsoundly based upon seven weeks' intuition in the USA.

The majority of Americans I met socially I found to be childlike, equipped with rather more than the usual number of national and personal prejudices, inclined to assess all things— motor-cars and nations—with an uneasy blend of emotion and economics. I found that they tended to avoid standards based on intellect. They did not seem to be very good at thinking, largely, I suppose, through lack of practice rather than through any national defect in mentality.

Of even the beginnings of the minutest embryo of a homogeneous culture there was no sign: there was a general reaction of bewilderment (not unmixed with pity) whenever it was tentatively suggested that knowledge and appreciation might be acquired for their own intrinsic values, rather than as catalysts for the amassing of bullion, respectability or washing-machines. Education, therefore, is economic and expedient— four or five subjects, such as brewing, real estate, creative-writing (God save the mark!) and angling, are taken by each student. This *mélange* is styled a 'liberal education', meaning that a student is permitted to know nothing about four things, instead of something about one. Accent is on the dispensing of economically useful information (sound Marxist doctine, that!) and not at all upon the development of the mind as a thinking unit. Thus, the American student inclines to statements that are dogmatic and unoriginal: he has an implicit and almost mediaeval trust in Authority.

(*October 11, 1950*)

Writing in Isis *after similar American tours, others did not always share Robinson's caustic opinion:*

The evening began with dinner, and often this would take place in a fraternity or sorority house. What a pleasant relaxation this was before the debate! They found, these debaters, that there was no better way of getting one's mind on to 'Nationalisation' for example, than to sit at table with up to sixty young American girls, all dressed up in the 'New Look,' and hanging on every word they said. They were the first Englishmen that these girls had met, and the Oxford accent in small doses is very attractive. 'Do you put it on?' asked one. The charm of a little naïvete in the sophisticated is fascinating. Thus the meal would pass all too quickly and the party adjourn to the auditorium. (Tony Benn, *February 25, 1948*)

A weekend with an all-female college at Atlanta introduced us to a severity of discipline unknown in any Oxford women's college. No smoking on campus. No drinking on campus. 'Dates' could be met and received only in 'date-parlours,' specially furnished rooms whose doors could never be closed. Our only vices were to blow bubblegum under careful instruction and to eat popcorn – accurately described to us as a form of granulated cardboard. (Robin Day, *January 18, 1950*)

110

Ooh! You Tease!
Oxford No Fun: Females Riot

Hideously mascara-ed and disguised in Dior gym-slips, *Isis* representatives swayed elegantly into St Hugh's for the inaugural debate of the recently formed Women's Debating Society [OU Inter-Collegiate Debating Association].

Amid cries of 'Natalie, you pinched my lakkers stick, you beast!' and much scuffling of feet, the deputising President announced the motion 'That this House deplores the Oxford way of life', and went on to say that everyone must put their shoulders to the grindstone and establish lots and lots of tradition, and if Muriel wouldn't keep quiet then she could just go outside!

Miss Shirley Catlin proposed the motion. Simpering prettily, she said she deplored the Oxford system of philosophy which gave her more than one answer to the same question: she coyly suggested Oxford be left to 'The Fellows'.

A little girl at the back started to cry, and was led out.

Miss Elizabeth Galbraith, opposing the motion, said how absolutely spiffing it was of Olive to cope so spiffingly with the job of president at five minutes' notice, and she was jolly sure everyone agreed it was spiffing. She said she liked Oxford because the bath-water was always hot.

Miss Caroline Mackintosh probably thought Palgrave's *Golden Treasury* was ripping, because she quoted nearly all of it. Miss Ann Chesney said the great thing about Oxford was that you might be going to be someone great, and consequently you could get away with a hell of a lot. Miss Marigold Robins thought the colleges were *lovely*, but full of horrid, horrid people.

A case of hair-pulling was rigorously dealt with by the President.

Just as the 'Ayes' were about to give tongue, a voice hissed: 'We *can't*: we'll wake the Principal.' A show of hands was called for. The President made it fifteen: a girl called Prudence said no it was seventeen. So the President said 'Hands up those who say it's fifteen!' Prudence said it jolly well wasn't fair. Another little girl started to cry. Everyone got up and started to wave their arms. Joyce Grenfell and Ronald Searle were seen to leave by side doors.

Suddenly someone shouted *'Cave!'*, and the room cleared like lightning.

(*October 26, 1949*)

Godfrey Smith *was President of the Oxford Union and a contributor to* The Isis. *He said relations between the two were bad but added in an article, 'when I had the misfortune to become involved in a public controversy,* The Isis *rallied splendidly to my aid with a resounding leading article.' On the death of Patrick Campbell, Smith took over his spot in the* Sunday Times, *contributing a weekly humorous column.*

The Ladies, Bless 'Em!

A reply to Robert Robinson's article on OUIDA

I felt very sad when I read Robert Robinson's article about the Women's Debating Society, but not, I suspect, for quite the same reason as other people. Indeed, very few people felt sad about it at all. The gusty laughter of BNC bruisers, with primevally low foreheads and shoulders four feet across, could be heard from Iffley Road all the way to the Parks: the faint echo of it reverberated sweatily round the walls of the Alfred Street Gymnasium days afterwards and disturbed the agonising birth of a corruscating editorial next door. 'Oh, what a hoot!' one heard them bellow; 'what a screech, what a scream! One up for the jolly old *Isis*, eh?' And one up it certainly was. No reflection on Robinson for doing his stuff. One can imagine him slinking into *The Isis* office, cowering away from the dark corner where the Editor sits harsh and austere in Mongolian isolation, for all the world like a cocaine-sodden and gin-soaked Under-Commissar for Cultural Affairs only to be brought sharply to heel by the familiar but still terrifying croak from that vice-ridden larynx. 'Robinson,' croaks the larynx forbiddingly, 'get me 850 words on the Women's Debate. And make it so funny that even the epsilon minuses in the Trinity JCR lie frothing with hysterical laughter on their lush-carpeted floors, and nicely-mannered Wykehamists in New College drum the ground with their genteel heels in uncontrolled paroxysms of delight.' Robinson pads off obediently into the night, and next Wednesday morning six thousand masculine hearts glow proudly over the morning kipper in hall to know that, here, at any rate, Man is still supreme. After all, it stands to reason, doesn't it? The jolly old *Isis* said it, so it *must* be true.

Let us delve, briefly into Robinson's past. First, let me say, I have nothing against Robinson personally. I think he is an able and entertaining journalist. The stuff about the Christian Dior gym tunics was incontrovertibly good. No, it lies deeper than that. It lies far, far, in the past, and not only, of course, in Robinson's past alone, but in all our yesterdays. For Robinson read Everyman if you have a leaning towards Morality.

As soon as the infant Robinson could begin to toddle and make intelligible sounds, and as soon as he could don the first minute polo jumper (the first of a long and increasingly grubby line), he was thrust into violent contact with Woman. Who knows what incalculable harm was done by that cute little number in the pink booties even before he was safely away from the nursing home? But, so far back, it is all haze and supposition. What is reasonably certain is that the young Robinson went to school. And here the Octopus of Good Form wrapped its greedy tentacles around him and engulfed him. 'Robinson,' said the Id craftily to him one day. 'You see that blonde in the teashop on the corner?' 'Yes,' said Robinson's Ego suspiciously, 'what about her?' 'Exactly,' said the Id insidiously, '*what* about her?' 'Id,' said Robinson's Ego pompously, drawing himself to his full height, 'you are perfectly disgusting and obscenely un-English. I shall never speak to you again.' And he never has. That is why poor Robinson is in the state he is today. Oh, of course there have been lapses. There was that dreary dance at the end of term when all those awful women from St Agatha's Sixth Form came across, but really, what chance was there for the Id between two orangeades and the ample form of the St Agatha's hockey mistress? So, you see, poor Robinson came up to Oxford with a stiff upper lip; and an unflinching determination to hate all women and to scamper from the swish of a skirt as he would from the clappers of hell.

His elder brother had come home in the vacs. with a cigarette holder and a copy of *Christopher Hobhouse*. This book was avidly devoured by young Robinson, who found in it the final vanquishment of that infernal but ever-recurrent bounder, his unspeakable Id. He learnt eagerly that Oxford women were pimply, wore shapeless tweeds, pedalled furiously from lecture to lecture, drank Nescafé in their silly little chintz-curtained rooms, and became French mistresses eventually in Birmingham. For nobody in the world is so eager in encouraging this ostracism than the soured and embittered Senior Common Room. Anyway, that was all young Robinson wanted to know. Of course, the Id would keep creeping slily into his imaginings—else where did he get that image of the languid Fashion Editress he is so sure of meeting in 1956 when they are both on the *Daily Express*? Or that beautiful yet passionate woman novelist with whom he will dance romantic Sambas in a Cheyne Walk luxury flat in 1958? 'Oh,' says Robinson to himself, 'they're *different*; they're *real, turbulent, dynamic* not like these'—and he turns his scathing wit in full measure upon luckless OUIDA, on its first difficult and quite unromantic struggle for self-expression.

For Robinson, alas, there is now no turning back, no half-way between the Femme Fatale he is positive he will one day meet at Biarritz and the embryo French Mistress at Lady Margaret Hall. He will pursue his romantic chimera until the end of his days, and, forty years on, in the Athenaeum, with his back to the fire and a whisky in his hand, he will still be pouring out his scintillating but now alas slightly middle-aged invective against The Ladies, God Bless 'Em. For there is no surer sign of the latent male wish to dominate than the laconic phrase

'The Ladies'. Here we are, all chaps together, and once a week, we have in the Ladies. How could he understand Shaw's heartcry in *Candida*—'Don't you understand what a woman *is?*'

For Robinson, as I have said, there seems to be little hope. For the benefit of young men still in their first enraptured term, I would append a list of words which they must never, never use, all the time they are here:

> Hobhouse
> Tweeds
> Nescafé
> Bicycles
> Lectures

but they will be able to think of more for themselves. Perhaps it is not too late for poor Robinson, if he makes a really *determined* effort now. Would he take a stub of pencil in an ink-stained finger and write down the following reading list as I dictate? Thank you.

> Dr Marie Stopes: *What Every Boy Should Know* (7/6d)
> Virginia Woolf: *A Room of One's Own* (8/6d)
> Beatrice Webb: *Our Partnership* (15/-)

Those will do to be going on with. We must all be very kind and not ask Robert out to *any* parties while he is reading, all agog, through his preliminary list. After all, who knows? It may make *all* the difference to him. No longer doomed to grumpy and middle-aged bachelordom, who can foretell what heights . . .

(*November 9, 1949*)

Elizabeth **Jennings** *studied English at St Anne's College. In the Fifties, she was hailed as one of the 'Movement' poets, while an assistant at Oxford City Library, from where she continued to write for* The Isis.

A View of Positano

He builds the town, puts houses random down
Though they have stood there long. But this is new,
He brings the angles narrow on the view,
Cracked plaster peels, breaks under sun, its rind
Composing then, and white within his mind.

The maps, sunglasses and binoculars
Are to detach the place from what he makes it,
To hold it off there in a clear perspective
And out of reach, placed apt in all particulars.
This needful to the town for staring fakes it

And leaves too personal a spirit there.
Afterwards, from the sea, it will grow dim
But rich in promises and seem to air
Its meaning publicly. Be as before
White houses fallen down the cliff
But rooted there as in no traveller's dream.

(October 15, 1952)

117

Reginald Bosanquet, *who became Britain's most controversial newscaster, joined the fledgling ITN as a trainee after leaving Oxford. He resigned in 1979. Bosanquet wrote, 'I loved Oxford but I often wondered why I bothered to do any work there. Nobody has ever asked me what degree I obtained.' He was stripped of his scholarship by New College because he decided to get married.*

Eccentrics

One of the chief reasons why Oxford today has lost something of the quality we associate with the Oxford of yesterday is the lack of great eccentrics. This is not the undergraduate's fault. Having, in so many cases, just exchanged his battledress for books he is entitled to expect a little more than he finds. Reluctantly but inevitably, during the first few weeks he becomes resigned to the narrowness of the subjects he may read, the lack-lustre quality of the lectures he may attend. But, even when this pill has been sugared, there still remains the lack of obvious eccentrics. This is no idle protest: if we do not heed the warning, learning will become sterile and the soul of Oxford will fly from the City.

Every evening at five I have sat in my window and watched college lawns fiercely hoping to see a figure emerge at that hour from the quadrangle and pass slowly into the garden where, prodding the grass and the worms with his stick, I might hear him mutter 'Ye've not got me yet, dam ye!' But he has never come; perhaps it is the wrong time of year, or perhaps he has already been. Where is the Fellow-for-life whose passage to chapel in the evening might be arrested by whistling at him? Where the lecturer who, having sat in silence, squat-legged like a buddha upon his desk for fifteen minutes, raised his eyes to consider his puzzled class and murmur 'Time passes,' pronouncing the 'a' hard? Have they gone too? and if so what of those who have taken their places? Do not the dons of today realise the immense burden of responsibility that has fallen to them? How many eyes seek eagerly some sign, some fleeting show of irregularity on their part? But as many are left to find it in a tie or a coat or a wilful neglect of clothes—in all the outward trappings, but never in the inward promise. If they are really gone, then we have witnessed the passing of a great comedy: its passing into a great tragedy.

How do they feel, those ghosts of the past, when they gather to consider the gentlemen who walk within their walls today? Were you to rise one morning very early when the mist lays comfortably about the college buildings, you might see in the grey end of darkness a silent assemblage of insubstantial Wardens and Fellows of the college, standing stock still, each watching a new generation come to life in the rooms about him. Then as the mists swirled together for a moment, there might break from one of the windows, hoarse at first but gaining in volume, a rowing song from Harvard—Mr Rhodes' unwitting contribution to the moment—and when you looked again they would have gone.

Eccentricity should have as much a part in a cultural community as the books it reads and the lectures it hears. One should go to a man's lectures as well for what he is discussing as for the way he talks; or for the possibility that he will not appear in the lecture hall at all, but be found some hours later discoursing to a wide-eyed child on the wonders of the Roman civilisation at Byzantium. The man who says he does not like mathematics is the man who has never been shown with what ease figures may be made to confound one another; even so may the pomposities of education be brought into proportion by their translation through the ridiculous. I do not mean that we should laugh at what we are taught, but that we should have the opportunity to laugh at the way we are taught it.

I think it was Oscar Wilde who said Nature was so unnatural (the ring is authentic), and that is perfectly true, even if in most cases her work is tampered with by forces other than her own. Eccentrics, like great men, are born not made. They are perhaps the only logically developed people amongst us, for they have grown naturally along the lines intended for them. While we, accepting every benefit that science and social research have been able to heap upon us, have become that ideal product of a highly developed educational system—an ordinary thinking man. Clever sometimes, amusing on occasion, original seldom, but natural never. We are not as nature intended us. I have been thwarted in my desire never to be punctual, you have been prevented continually from eating your meals standing up (unquestionably an assistance to the digestion), and we have become in the process very ordinary people. There are a few who have not, but now they, like housemaids, are a dying race, and nobody has yet leapt forward to demand their preservation.

Form, at once, a Society for the Preservation of Genuine Eccentrics and restore to Oxford one of its oldest glories. But remember, my impulsive friend, that there is a quality of reticence about fine things that adds to their distinction, and do not seek to create false prophets or to shout your mission from the roof-tops. Do not even feel that you have to be honest about your intentions: mendacity is the morality of conceit, and you are not nearly sure enough of yourself to wish to be respectable. Remember that in the eccentric you are dealing with a sensitive and barely gregarious creature; act accordingly. But it is not for me to instruct you in your duties. Your understanding the need is sufficient proof of your ability.

It is probably unwise to say that any society depends for its balance upon a single thing, but in some cases it would be an injustice if this were not said. I would rather preserve one real eccentric and lose seventy 'normal' men, if by so doing I could temper a society that has in it enough of the weight of learning with something of the sublimely ridiculous. Here we are in constant danger of taking too seriously the attitude of not taking life seriously enough, and if we could be confronted from time to time with the assurance that life is not serious at all, we should gain inestimably from the encounter.

(October 29, 1952)

Less lack-lustre lectures

George Macbeth *was described as 'the most inventive poet of his generation in Britain'. His first book, published while still studying at New College in 1954,* A Form of Words, *is now a collectors' item.*

Rhubarb

Two thousand years beyond their time
Untutored in the art of scope
These plants repeat an old mistake.

Flora now buried under grime
Once healed the first expansive ache
And threw their drowning world a rope.

But vast exceptions past their prime
On wasted ground without real hope
Still like to grow for growing's sake.

Stones

Stones that are chiselled by the niggling rain,
Dislodged by blast, or twisted in the grain,
Sometimes attain a chaos of pure form,
The core of marble in the whirling storm.

Thus Chance may show where famous secrets hid,
The key to Sculpture in the conic lid,
The rhythmic metre of the pyramid.

(March 11, 1953)

Ned Sherrin, *who became a film, theatre and television producer, director and writer, was born in Somerset. He became undergraduate president of Exeter College and critical editor of* The Isis. *An 'Idol' described him as 'the publicist, the impresario, the man who gets things done'. In the theatre, it went on, his most noteworthy performance was as the Fairy Queen—'a bright spark in a tiresome pantomime'.*

My Home Town: Kingweston

Sitting under a cow during the vacation, I could see Kingweston 'up across'. A grey haze, a line of trees, a couple of thatched cottages, several clusters of brown-tiled roofs, three solid farms and an outsize steeple. It was hard to reconcile all this with an *Isis* feature; and 'my home town' recalls the painful exercises of E. Sherrin (aged 11½ years)—the 'autobiography of a grain of wheat', 'a day in the life of a penny', 'happiest day of my hols.'. Surely they didn't want that either. In his letter the man said, 'Something light and amusing about the agricultural township (I suppose that is what it is) of Kingweston.'

I will not snatch easy laughs from woad and worzels. My interest in Kingweston—though born of necessity—is deep. On the other hand, it is hard not to slip into whimsy and babble the names of green fields. There is a wood called Maggoty-Paggoty (it says so, too, on the 'one inch to the

124

mile'). A patch of arable is called Peace Close, and thirty acres of recent ley which have two names, Bushy Leary and Lark's Whistle. Bushy no longer, thanks to gyrotiller and bulldozer; Leary no more, thanks to plough and mole drain. I can remember beating my way through it at the age of ten, when it was the roughest scrub in the village. My brother had been given an air-gun for his birthday and the place was infested with rabbits. In 1953 it yielded hundreds of bales of hay.

Kingweston stands on the edge of the Blackmore Vale before it drops away into the King's Sedgemoor. There are no streets, street lamps, or public lavatories (there are several pumps and there is a telephone kiosk). Theoretically the cottages are numbered; but in fact old Mrs Lock's is distinguished from young Mrs Lock's because everyone knows that the latter is Mrs Stan's, and who would go to Mrs Stan if they wanted old Mrs George? One cottage had a nameplate for a time, but if it remains it is a monument to the folly of ideas above one's station and not as an address.

The village has remained a unit, and even if there is less significance in a social hierarchy today, the unit which followed automatically on that hierarchy has not entirely disappeared. It is too early to judge how radically village life has changed. It had changed little at the beginning of the war. Stability is only just returning. There are many signs that the younger generation may show that the country character is a more important influence on their behaviour than modern developments.

Kingweston has no cinema, no pub and no shop. At least, the post office sells Sharp's toffee, Fox's glacier mints, tobacco and envelopes and has an early closing day (Wednesdays); but despite all these qualifications it is not a shop proper. The village is of course all the better for having none of these things. It has no vice, either. Illegitimacy is rarely finally ascertained, no matter how much comment a characteristic nose on the wrong face may excite; and 'anomalies' are not talked about, so I don't know.

There are, of course, other entertainments. There is, once a year, a whist drive for the Cricket Club. There used to be another for the Organ Fund, but as we now have an organ it was impossible to find any excuse for carrying it on. A country

125

whist drive requires only one line in conversation. 'If you 'aven't got the cards, you can't make the tricks, can 'ee?'

The farm-worker of today is very much the same as he was before the war; perhaps not the same as he was at the turn of the century; but in reality football pools and excursion tours have rarely made more than a superficial impression. Yet, this is not surprising, for though his work may be harder than that of most, he usually realises his unique advantages as well. He will not admit them and has indeed come to regard them as a right—but they make attractive reading to people who do not know about them. From wages of around £6 a week, no more than a few shillings—perhaps 3/- are taken by rent; nothing for milk, water, cider, installation of electricity, vegetables and all the other necessities. There is plenty of room for gardens and allotments and for keeping poultry. It is not an unattractive prospect, as those who leave the village to try to equate a bigger pay packet with a more expensive council house find out.

Politically Kingweston is traditionally Conservative. The agricultural unions are not strong there. However, there is a growing tendency in the countryside to think twice rather than to vote automatically. Politics are rarely a burning question now. The days when they painted Bert Spicer's donkey blue have gone, and so has a good deal of the irresponsibility that went with them.

Somerset dialect is more interesting than ever before. It is no longer a mummified remain. An independent language which has remained the same for generations is being subjected to outside influences. The study of dialect is no longer a work of preservation. The old picturesque phrases remain. Who would want to say, 'Was he drunk?' when the two alternatives are 'Did 'er ketch 'un one?' and 'Did 'er hab'n on?' Side by side with these walk the new slickisms of the cinema; but they are all settling in, if they are useful and help you to say what you mean.

It is generally accepted by townsfolk that the countryman is unintelligent. This is not true. It is true to say that he moves in a different gear. Everything depends on agriculture; and life is conditioned by the land. It is difficult to rush nature even with new inventions. (Incidentally, the best farmer is always the second person to buy a new implement.) Coming back to Somerset, it is difficult to change down at first; after a week or so it is inevitable. Townsmen periodically arrive and try to hurry things. They either leave or slow down more happily. The clever man is of course the one who can keep changing gear, but this is a luxury and there is no good reason why the countryman should indulge in it . . .

Under the cow with the sun coming, the dew going and the mist compromising, all this seemed very valid. But the cow moved and the milk refused to flow, and I found that in trying to sum up a village I too had got into the wrong gear myself, and the sooner the change was made the better.

(January 27, 1954)

Christopher Ricks *studied English at Balliol College and became Professor of English at Cambridge. Perhaps his most famous work is* Milton's Grand Style.

A Writer's Craftiness

I wasn't very surprised to see Nathaniel Gland at The Rough Rood, but I was surprised that he should speak to me, in fact, more, leave the circle which so agreeably hemmed him in, and come across the room. The Rough Rood is one of those select pubs which are said to be the regular meeting places of famous men in literature or Fleet Street. I had been hanging around it in the lunch-hour for about a week, in the hope of finding a publisher or patron sufficiently drunk to be kind, but sufficiently sober to appreciate my talent, shown in conversation or in my slightly grubby, too-long-folded manuscripts. I had seen no Christopher Fry and no John Lehmann, but anyway here was Nathaniel Gland. I had last seen him at Oxford a few years ago, but it would be pointless to pretend I had ever really known him there. He had already been a name, and young enough for 'promising' to be a compliment, and I remember the absurd pleasure I received when he called me by my Christian name, at a meeting of the Crabbe Society, I believe. Now he was even more affable. 'How delightful to see you again,' he said, 'I had no idea you used this place', and nudged me towards his companions. I murmured that I didn't want to intrude, and let myself be persuaded to join them.

As I looked at the eager and earnest disciples, I thought how little Gland's situation had changed since he was up at Oxford. There too he had generally been surrounded. The discussion was similarly deferential, and a young man was saying rather diffidently 'But surely the fundamental point is whether Spleen *in itself* is a sign of the fanatic. You remember what Camus said . . .' So my thoughts wandered. Nathaniel Gland had never been a crude exhibitionist at Oxford. His initial skill had lain in his acquiring a most pervasive reputation as a writer when no one had ever actually seen anything of his in print. He was always seen clutching great bundles of paper, which we were allowed to assume were his manuscripts, and he flatteringly asked people's advice. Since he knew that most literary criticism at Oxford is mere destruction, he saw the need not to give any chance to would-be attackers. I think he thought of himself as of a Professor of Poetry; because of his very authority and value, he was to be exposed to danger as rarely as possible. But after a time it was obvious that he could not remain famous on the skill of his not-writing. He realised, though, that it was essential not to be published for the first time in a university magazine. He wrote energetically, and even more energetically telephoned friends and relations. Then he had a poem accepted in *Gripe*. The poem was as short as was compatible with poetic existence and decency. It very much resembled those oddities which Blunden still sends home marked 'A Present From Japan'. Gland then wrote his only contribution to an undergraduate magazine. It avoided the facetious vein of the very bad Fourth Leader, which even then was depressingly omnipresent; instead it dealt in a scholarly but vigorous way with the implication of Cambridge's abolition of the mortar-board. Had it not been studded with 'so to speak' and 'as it were', it would have been difficult to believe Gland had actually written it.

The idea which really made his name, though, was a simple but original one. Instead of being, like most, a monotonous poseur, month after month the same, he would devote each week to one great literary figure. Imitation would be the sincerest form of homage. At first, he had intended to choose from all ages, and he began with Dr Johnson. He started every aphorism (he spoke almost exclusively in aphorisms) with 'Sir', and finished it with 'and there's an end on't'. He drank tea instead of coffee, made himself uncomfortable by taking snuff, and hired a Boswell. But he was forced to admit failure; his crass rudeness and his scorn of clean linen made him, not distinct, but absolutely indistinguishable from the mass of undergraduates from whom he had expected attention. He had the sense to change his mind, and limited his field to contemporary literature, a decision which made his performance more hazardous and also more interesting, since quite often one had no idea whom he was imitating. 'Guessing Gland' became a popular way of killing time at lectures. I remember a particularly amusing week which began when all his old acquaintances, even the slightest, like myself, received a most odd letter. Mine began, 'Dear ole Kenneth Graham(e) Green', and continued with many capital letters, swear words, exclamation marks, dogmatic statements about contemporary writers and frequent misquotations, especially from the Chinese, it seems. Ezra Pound Week had begun. It was one of Gland's most successful.

I was brought back to The Rough Rood by a bright youth who had presumably taken *Macbeth* for Prelims., and who said 'I suppose his dull brain is wrought with things forgotten.' Gland managed a smile which was somehow properly chiding.

Fortunately he was by this time tired of holding court in The Rough Rood, and a royal hint dispersed his attendants. I mentioned that perhaps I ought to go too; no, he said, he wanted a long chat with me. He had always valued my opinion, he said, and knew I wasn't a silly ducking observant. I saw that he still had both his former near-giggle when he quoted anything, and his wish for flattery.

'What are you doing these days?' I asked, 'apart from your work for *The Prattler*, of course'. 'Well, at the moment I'm working on what I hope will be a new Ars Poetica, or anyway, Art Poétique. But it's got to be a work of art itself. Sounds a bit pompous, I'm afraid. Here. Let me show you what I mean', and he fumbled for a piece of paper and then wrote quickly. I read:

130

'It is no mystery,
Technical mastery,
Just trudging drudgery
One mustn't grudge.'

Of course, it's still in pretty rough shape', Gland said hurriedly, 'but I expect you can see what I'm after. I suppose you've noticed the different thicknesses of that u-sound which seems to be always the same; you know, the shadows they cast backwards and forwards. What did Edith Sitwell say?—something about assonances so subtle they are almost dissonances, or was it the other way round?' 'Yes, should be most interesting. When do you expect to get it out by?' 'Unfortunately I've got a couple of bread-and-butter jobs I must get done first. One must live, you know.' I agreed mentally. He went on. 'I expect you remember I was always interested in Jasper Mayne?' I didn't, and he leant closer. 'Anyway the fact is that those seventeenth-century poets—or is he eighteenth?—anyhow, they're an absolute gift. I mean the very minor ones. Nobody knows anything about them except that they ought to admire them. I'm producing a volume of Mayne sometime next month I hope, and I think I've hooked twenty minutes to talk about him on the Third. All I want now is a commission to do a Penguin—say, Contemporary European Verse, yes, with translations. I'd commission you to do half a dozen translations', he added generously. Soon after, we parted on that friendly note, with a probability of meeting in a fortnight's time.

Looking back I can see that that evening was probably near Gland's zenith. Had I thought so at the time, I would not have kept hidden my manuscripts or plans for literary advancement, but I thought the next meeting would be more opportune. I had intended to be a journalist, but the fact that I had never engaged in undergraduate journalism had not quite been sufficient qualification. I am even now surprised at the swiftness of Gland's fall. But he looked very worried when I next met him, and he had obviously been drinking. He came quickly to the point. He had woken up one morning to find himself completely incapable of writing a word; he had no ideas, he couldn't think of anything at all to write, and even if he could

131

have, he was sure he wouldn't be able to put it down on paper. He now admitted that lately his writing had been fluent to the point of glibness, and now, suddenly, this awful drying-up, like an actor who had played a part thousands of times. 'And I've got to send a short story to *Excelsior* sometime today,' he moaned. Then he asked cunningly, 'Have you written any short stories lately?' 'But surely you must have dozens of stories ready to send in?' I asked in reply. 'I had, but I've used them all in the last week. Have you got any?' 'Yes, but nobody could possibly think they were yours; it's very flattering of you, but . . .'—'Don't worry about that,' he interrupted, 'have you got any on you?' With a show of reluctance I handed him the few I had, and he skimmed through them. I felt bound to point out that they were not fashionable short stories, atmospheric descriptions of kitchens, mothers and children, but that they tried, however unsuccessfully, to tell a story. He grunted, and chose one. 'This'll do,' he said, 'fifty-fifty with the money?' He obviously wasn't as drunk as I'd thought. 'I did write the story,' I began. 'Oh yes, but would it ever be published except under my name?' he asked all too pertinently, and so I agreed. As he left, he mumbled, 'Must keep my name in front of the public. Absolutely essential.'

Clearly though, my being able to write was no real cure for his being, practically speaking, struck illiterate. Neither of us liked the arrangement, as we both thought it debased us, or anyway lost us money. I couldn't keep up anything like the Gland rate for writing short stories, and I was completely unable to produce a poem of more than half a dozen lines which would bear any resemblance to his. Gland became desperate when I told him we would have to drop the whole thing. Keeping his name before the public became the only thing that mattered. He wrote letters, virulent and exaggerated letters, to every possible newspaper and magazine. When one day I saw that he was looking less worried than usual, I questioned him at once. 'You must be able to write again, surely?' 'No,' he snapped, 'but I've got what may be a big chance to create a stir—to give them the old Gland magic; I've got that twenty minutes on the Third Programme.'

In the interlude which preceded his talk, I listened to the Extracts from the Diaries of the Rev. Thomas Pinkin (1759-

1825) without granting them their wonted attention. I sensed that this evening would be Nathaniel Gland's turning-point. He began quietly enough, but it was deceptive. He lulled the gentlemen of the BBC into casualness, and then sprang from a discussion of Jasper Mayne and his modern critics into a discussion of the modern critics, in particular of their morals. Rapidly after the critics followed the writers, publishers and especially editors. By the time the engineers finally got Gland off the air, he had slandered most of England's eminent literary figures. And he had created a stir.

He lost a great deal of money and his job on *The Prattler*. Ironically enough, his fluency, with tongue and pen, had returned for that fatal evening, and is still with him. But now he could no longer be trusted. I have said his fall was swift, and it was. For soon after he won an Honourable Mention in *The Sunday Times* Short Story Competition, and nowadays I see Nathaniel Gland granted in a magazine a small uncomfortable space between Godfrey Winn and Beverley Nichols.

(June 2, 1954)

Anthony Howard *became President of the Oxford Union on his second attempt. He is currently deputy editor of* The Observer, *having edited both the* New Statesman *and* The Listener. *The 1955* Isis *'Idol' said his intense desire for success led to 'his refusal to do anything at which he is not certain of doing well'.*

Changing Scene

No one would voluntarily choose the career of the Spanish street beggar whose solitary and supreme object in life is to gain a few pence of pity by the public exhibition of his wounds. And as I take Mr Levy seriously, my aim in writing this article is not to gain an apprenticeship in that particular trade. I must plainly try to be a hearty, expansive extrovert—like those gay people who appear in the by now familiar block at the top of this page. Picture me, then, appearing next term wielding an experienced oar or waving a well-worn cocktail glass. But before that fate (naturally worse than death) overtakes me there are two things which I expressly want to do. The first is to be like the small-time local politician on the balcony of the Town Hall and thank all the people who voted for me, as well as congratulating those many more who did not. And the second is to try to administer some benzedrine to the usual platitudes that are inevitably uttered by the loser about the victor. In a way that is easy; for mercifully I cannot be caught in the gin trap of all the old clichés about 'good clean fight', 'fair, hard-hitting struggle', 'contest in which proud to have taken part'. There was not really any contest, very little struggle and certainly no fight. Anyway, so far as Jeremy Isaacs and I were concerned the election was probably more of a co-operative endeavour than a competitive enterprise. And I should like to say here what I am too shy to say privately—that if anyone is more fortunate than the Union in its President for next term then it is the writer of this article in having had in him such a generous, maternal and model opponent.

Everyone who has been defeated for the Presidency of the Union—and there are quite a lot of us by now (some comfortingly distinguished)—must, I imagine, on the day after the result feel rather like Humpty Dumpty off the wall. Everything seems to be in bits and one wonders whether one will ever be able to piece it all together again. The real trouble of course is that the delusion of grandeur, which even H. Dumpty must have had when he sat on top of his wall, is at an end. You feel rather like Mr Stan Johnson who, you may remember, wrote this article a fortnight ago, and was in a terribly bad way (poor chap) because, as he told us, his 'dreams had vanished in the morning light'. That, I suppose, is largely how life seems to a Presidential candidate the morning after the night before. He was left the previous evening alone in monumental mockery on top of the band-waggon, and the only ladder down—right down to the bottom—was drink.

But however dislocated, and perhaps dissipated, one feels, there was, at least in my case, something which stood out above all the oddly conflicting emotions with which I was contorted, and that was that it had been worth it. It wasn't just fun while it lasted; it is still fun, if only in retrospect, now it has finished. I don't know what is the attraction—the elation, the excitement or simply the experience. But whatever it is, it must be fairly strong; for it prevails over the cremation of ambition, the creation of disappointment and the creature defects of the flesh like lack of sleep and loss of appetite. And the greatest tribute of its strength that I know is the fact that we nearly all, if we have the chance, go through the whole hell over again even though we realise that however much we press forward the prize of the calling is too high for our reach.

135

The result when it comes is an anti-climax—at any rate if it is the kind of result that I got. One has premonitions; and unhappily they prove to be right. Still, if I could choose where to hear it, it would be where in fact I did hear it—or rather saw it in a downcast averted look—at a Labour Club meeting. Everything is made so much easier when one has an audience; the knowledge that people are watching you represents the subtlest form of behaviour control that I know. It is very hard to weep on a collective shoulder; and anyway with an ex-Chancellor of the Exchequer talking merrily of public ownership and private profits this is fairly obviously not the way the world ends.

In fact by the end one has got beyond caring. All I wanted was for the result to come; and when it did, after the first moment of declaration of total war on God and man, I simply felt relief that it was all over. The worst period indeed was the days immediately preceding the Debate; only then, and only for a very brief time, was any strain placed upon my personal feelings towards the Man Between—and that was largely the result of an exuberant exercise in inimitable illiteracy which had appeared in the *Cherwell* a day or two before the election. Thursday morning itself came as a release; and I look back on Thursday evening after the Presidential Debate as my most recent recollection of contentment.

Friday—Election Day—was the oddest of the lot. The sentence we had imposed upon ourselves was exile from Oxford, so after a ritualistic, Demosthenic voting, we set out in a good popular Ford (as befitted Friends of The People) for an unknown destination. It turned out to be Burford; the fact that there is a good fast flowing river there and that the President Elect of the Union can't swim may have had something to do with it. The intention had been a fine, strapping Salopian country walk; but instead the afternoon transformed itself into brandies, brandies, all the way. At one moment it looked as if we would be marooned on the top of the Cotswolds, not because of the brandies but, unromantically, because of a fog. The decision as to who should walk and who should stay with the car became a matter of some delicacy. But in the end furious driving from me and furious smoking from him (a not very helpful activity in the prevailing atmosphere)

136

got us back.

After that—well, you know the rest; and though it is no doubt an excellent spiritual purgative for me to remember it, it offends my aesthetic sense of how things should be. So let's leave it at that—and eat, drink and be merry for next term again we die. It is only the scene that changes; the people— even the successful ones—remain as they were.

(*December 1, 1954*)

Adrian Mitchell *was editor of* The Isis *and president of the poetry society in Oxford. He made his acting debut as Fourth Crowdsman in an existentialist production of* Julius Caesar—*a performance which led* Evening News *critic Felix Barker to describe him as 'a Harpo Marx-like character'. Isis 'Idol' portrayed him as 'polo-necked and articulating, in a bar or a street or in his higgledy-piggledy room, noisy and delighted, amply gesturing as he tells a story'. He says he still stands by his editorial 'Dream'.*

Dream

'It was in a city street. A baby sat, lolling against its mother's shins, in a sunlit doorway. The child was dressed in knitted white; it was plump under its socks and gloves and small pullover. Its head was gently covered with the same white wool. Only its face was uncovered. It stared out of its right eye. The left side of its face was made of rusty metal, a jagged line ran down the nose where metal and flesh joined. The left eye was a thick, empty circle. I knew that there had been some sort of explosion.'

That was a dream, and there was no anger in it. There was no need for anger, for there was nothing to be done, except pity. Dreams are supposed to blur and disappear, but the city and the street, the mother and the child are still clear-cut, and the rough surface of the corroding metal cheek is still tangible. Any pity that was given then is still as necessary, though the savaged child may seem a trivial figure among so many dead. It is easy to help this child, to show it compassion, and then to walk out of the front door proudly. It is difficult to make this child, its suffering and the responsibility for its mutilation and inevitable death, our own. Perhaps it is even harder to do all in our slight power to prevent the next death.

In war it is easy to forget the child, and to see the victims of our ferocity as faceless giants, mad and evil. We are told that we kill for the sake of our freedom, and that this is a noble and unselfish action. Our enemies are told the same, and they too believe it. Or we are told that we kill for the sake of the freedom of others. (Though Germany's attempted conquest of Europe was well advanced before we intervened in 1939.) Freedom is our clear cry, and for its sake we are prepared to throw away our integrity, and all but the old pretence of morality.

This is an atrocity, not a fairy story, for there is no villain and no hero in war. It is not worth going through hell for the promised Princess, she is cruel and old. It may be morbid to thumb endlessly through the horrors of war, but it woud be unrealistic to forget that human bodies are deliberately maimed, blinded and torn to pieces like useless sheets of paper; that each death in war is a murder. As our allegiance to the human race is greater than our loyalty to any government, our duty is clear. We must refuse to kill, knowing that this decision does not wash us clean of responsibility or guilt. We cannot cut ourselves from the State at war, but we can refuse to inflict suffering deliberately.

The pacifist is one who has examined the obscene instrument of war and rejected it as both impractical and immoral. He cannot accept the conventional picture of Alexander, Julius Caesar and Napoleon Bonaparte as great men. To him the refusal to go to war is not a negative gesture, it is an assertion of humanity. Eugene V. Debs said at his trial: 'I am opposed to war. I am perfectly willing on that account to be branded as a traitor . . . Years ago I recognised my kinship with all living beings, and I made up my mind that I was not one whit better than the meanest of earth. I said then, and I say

139

now, that while there is a lower class, I am in it; while there is a criminal element, I am of it; while there is a soul in prison, I am not free.' Those are the words of a man who had begun to love his neighbour and his enemy, who knew that the bad dream need not recur indefinitely. We may say that they are the words of a great man, for man is as great as his love.

(February 9, 1955)

David Marquand *became a Labour MP, but then joined the SDP in 1981. He went to Magdalen College from Emmanuel School. He said on hearing of the anthology, 'I think I got more fun out of writing for* Isis *than out of anything else I did at Oxford.'*

The Hapsburgs of Clapham Junction

'And I hope you will all join the Old Boys' Association. The subscription is only 10s 6d a year . . .'

The Headmaster shook hands, and we left, free but deflated. Ten minutes earlier we had filed suspiciously into his study, uncertain what was coming, but sure it would be (at least in intention) solemn, admonitory, uplifting—a sex-warning perhaps; a condemnation of the materialism that was sapping the foundations of our moral values; an attack, even, on the LCC. No one expected the unemotional sales talk we did get; and it was a let-down.

In a way, this was typical of the school. It was a squat brick building, vaguely mock Tudor, about ten minutes' walk from Clapham Junction station. From the drive it looked quite impressive—like the schools we used to read about in the *Rover* and *Champion*. Ivy grew with dignified profusion down the walls; in the distance you could see the tops of rugby goal posts. A transatlantic visitor, unfamiliar with the delicate convolutions of English snobbery, might have been tempted

141

to think it one of the Stately Schools of England. This temptation would have been strengthened if he had gone in through the main entrance: on the wall in front of him he would have seen a plaque announcing defiantly that the school had been founded in 1592.

Nevertheless, the transatlantic visitor would have been wrong. In the struggle between 1592 and Clapham Junction, Clapham Junction was an easy winner. The Tudor style of the buildings symbolised the pretentiousness of the school itself. Its pupils included one or two intellectual snobs and a sprinkling of juvenile delinquents. But most of them were the sons of publicans, small shopkeepers, tax collectors, local government officials—the backbone of Britain. There were a few working-class children and a few from the professional class. But these were out-numbered by the mass of South London Micawberdom from the shabby-genteel houses of the surrounding boroughs—Battersea, Clapham, Wandsworth, Tooting—speaking the refined cockney of SW18. But despite Clapham Junction, the school had pretensions. The Headmaster constantly referred to it as a Public School. Some of the masters believed him.

The buildings were honeycombed with long, dark, tortuous corridors, hideously decorated in light brown or chocolate distemper. In a normal day one walked for miles in the semi-darkness, from classroom to classroom, pursued by an unidentified smell of boiled vegetables and the noise of the trains. The general air of dilapidation and decay—occasionally relieved by half-hearted and futile attempts to brighten the place up—reflected (perhaps had even been originally responsible for) the ineffectuality and muddle of the school administration. It was like the Hapsburg or Romanov monarchy in decay. A Headmaster is bound to be a despot—either benevolent, malevolent, or just ineffectual. Ours was ineffectual. Power was constantly shifting from him to a clique of the more energetic of the staff, and then, as belatedly he reasserted himself, back again. Political advancement demanded the trimming ability and delicate intuitions of the expert in Soviet *fraktionspolitik*. This presented budding historians with a test tube specimen of the distribution of power under the decaying autocratic regimes, and those with a taste for machine politics with delightful opportunities for intrigue. But it did not lead to good government.

The nobility of this *Ancien Régime* were the prefects—privileged but socially useless. We supervised lunch queues, checked those who arrived late in the mornings, and were able to make people come to detention on Saturdays. But the jobs we did were either unnecessary, or could have been better done by the masters (who were too lazy to do them). The real reason for becoming a prefect was to have a study where you could smoke undetected, to be able to come late in the morning yourself, and to wear a trilby hat instead of a school cap. (This was for some reason a valuable privilege—wearing school caps was the most hated burden of the unprivileged). Since the system on which prefects were appointed was chaotic and uncertain—only members of the First XV were prefects by right—to become a prefect involved considerable intrigue and angling for position. (It was a good training for a career in an Oxford political club.) And though the prefects were on the whole kindly and did not take themselves very seriously—Russian nobles rather than Prussian junkers—they did not justify themselves or make the administration run more smoothly.

This general muddle and inefficiency irritated the tidy minded—the Hapsburg Empire must have infuriated those whose political ideal is that the trains should run on time. But it was a pleasanter regime to live under than a dynamic, efficient one would have been. This was particularly obvious in summer. After the GCE examinations were over, the school field was littered with recuperating examinees, playing cards, talking, or just lying peacefully in the sun. This drove the Headmaster frantic. He would rush out at periodic intervals from his study and chase the sunbathers back into the classrooms. But he couldn't keep them there. When he had gone back they would come back, and an hour later the whole comedy would have to be re-enacted. 'You have not yet ploughed all the fields of human knowledge,' he told me once, interrupting a tense game of solo, 'and if you feel you have, then pack your bags and go—there is always Clarke's College.' (Clarke's College was a target of abuse only less favoured than the LCC—what it was or where it was I never found out.) But

143

we both knew that this was only a conventional move, imposed on him by his position, that after he had gone back to his study I would strip to the waist again and go on with the game, and that in fact I wouldn't pack my bags and go to Clarke's College. In fact if I had wanted to pack my bags and go, no one would have been more distressed than the Head: in some complicated way his salary depended on the number of boys in the school above a certain age, and sixth-formers were rumoured to be worth ten shillings a week per head to him.

Other people's schooldays seem to have played a vital part in their lives, to have twisted their psyches and left scars which will never be effaced. Mine played almost no part. They were vacant, eventless, and in retrospect on the whole delightful: I am prepared to forgive a lot for the opportunity of sunbathing all summer.

(March 7, 1956)

144

Sylvia Plath, an American and a poet, studied at Newnham College, Cambridge, in the mid-Fifties. She committed suicide in 1963. Her piece in The Isis *was part of an occasional series of contributions from the rival university.*

Cambridge Letter

'Guess Where It's Heaven to be a Girl!' the *Woman's Sunday Mirror* gushed a short while back; we couldn't, so read on. Cambridge University, it seems, is this very green Eden, offering women students 'a crazy mixed-up social whirl, with an average of 500 bottle parties per eight week term.' Slightly staggered by such statistics as 'In her 45 weeks at Cambridge she has had 180 dates with 45 different men', we skimmed through an account of dating life that would have made the Alpha maidens in *Brave New World* take to soma, wild with envy.

Varsity, admitting that the *Mirror* account contained nothing 'specifically untrue', cleverly criticised the exaggerated effect arising from the 'subtle technique of leaving out'. Leaving out, no doubt, those bluestockinged Cambridge women who brood in the University Library until closing time. Or also, the advice given by the main speaker at a women's college dinner: cloister yourself in 'research' during these three precious academic years; avoid, if possible, anything so distracting as summer jobs: 'You can always get out in the world later.'

Fresh from the easy-going co-educational school system in America, where boys and girls are not immured in segregated public schools during adolescence until they come upon the 'opposite sex' with some of the self-consciousness and awe of an amateur anthropologist confronting, for the first time, a mob of orangoutangs (or vice versa), we paused to reflect upon the position of women in Cambridge, upon the man/woman relationship, even.

Apparently, the most difficult feat for a Cambridge male is to accept a woman not merely as feeling, not merely as thinking, but as managing a complex, vital interweaving of both. Men here are inclined to treat women in one of two ways: either (1) as pretty beagling frivolous things (or devastating bohemian things) worthy of May balls and suggestive looks over bottles of Chablis by candlelight, or, more rarely, (2) as esoteric opponents on an intellectual tennis court where the man, by law of kind, always wins.

Is this drastic split in the functions of a whole woman (matter versus mind, one might say) a flaw in the male approach, or does it stem from some lack on the woman's side? Perhaps a little of both. We shall deal, however, with the former. A debonair Oxford PPE man demurred, laughing incredulously: 'But really, talk about philosophy with a *woman*!' A poetic Cambridge chap maintains categorically: 'As soon as a woman starts talking about intellectual things, she loses her feminine charm for me.' By complaining about such remarks here, we are not advocating abstruse discussions about the animal symbolism in *The Garden of Delights* by Hieronymus Bosch, but only a more natural and frequent commerce between male and female minds on their favourite subjects; perhaps in supervisions, perhaps in coffee shops: a sense of fun, not artificial posturing, in playing with ideas where a woman keeps her female status while being accepted simultaneously as an intelligent human being.

In a society where men outnumber women ten to one, women are, admittedly, in an artificial position; competition is keen, even deadly, and the difficulty of acquiring a date induces many Cambridge men to draw on the reservoir of blonde, monosyllabic Scandinavian girls at the English schools, favouring what is often the prettier, less complicated, side of the pass.

Perhaps a restoration of the old French salon, with each Cambridge girl presiding like Madame Récamier over her ratio of ten men, would enrich male/female relationships. More likely, co-educational public schools would make intelligent sharing of ideas easier, less self-conscious from an earlier age. At least co-ed university activities such as political clubs, newspaper work, and acting, make it possible for men and women to meet on a sounder basis than the superficial sherry party where a girl is just that, and, alas, not much more.

(May 16, 1956)

Dennis Potter, according to Isis *in 1958, had 'crowned the achievement of previous editors in converting a smarties' haven into a serious journal'. At middle-class Oxford, the Gloucester miner's son 'boiled eggs in a tin kettle rather than dine in hall; he tried every stratagem to stop his scout calling him sir'. On leaving New College, he joined the current affairs department of the BBC, and later became a major television dramatist.*

Changes at the Top

At twenty-five past three in the afternoon the morning shift would crunch down the road that dropped through the village, their work over for the day. 'Evenings' came back at half-past eleven at night, and the others at six in the mornings, so this was the only returning shift you could see properly, and it was accordingly always something of an event in the day. The ponderous and out-of-step clamp, clamp, clamp of steel-toed pit boots could be heard minutes before the men came by, and I was able to rush to the wall, eager to see the coal-black faces, the corduroy trousers hitched and string-tied just below the padded knees, and the helmets shaped rather like those worn by the Nazi soldiers in my weekly copy of *The Champion* (the comic everyone seemed to take to supplement the *Daily*

Herald or the *Daily Mirror*). For me, and, I suspect, for the adults as well, those returning, grimy men up from the bowels of the earth had a peculiar glamour that inevitably disappeared when the pale, scrubbed faces and collars and ties came out later in the evening; anyway, most people came to the door when this shift passed, including the miserable-looking whippets, tails curved to a taper under their trembling tube-thin bodies.

My grandfather had silicosis after more than fifty years working at the coal face, yet he would always try and come to the wall, breathing so heavily that I was never quite sure whether he was laughing to himself, or humming some old tune. He could neither read nor write, nor remember the time before he went down the pit, so all his conversations were on this one theme, and he constructed elaborate pieces of invective about some event that had happened years before. He would invariably greet the first man by with a set question, and a little formalized dialogue would take place:

'And how's him been, butty?' ('Him' was the pit manager. This was occasionally re-phrased as 'the bastard', but without any particularly violent connotation, being used merely as an accepted and perfectly natural description.)

'Not too bad today, ol' un.' Pause. 'And how's your chest?'

'Middlin', middlin', butty.'

Only something as exciting as a severe accident at pit-bottom or a sudden change in the weather would upset the pattern of this conversation. The men were never very eager to stop and talk, since in their homes the tin baths had already been unhooked from the back-kitchen walls, and kettles would be boiling, ready for the scrub.

It is only when remembering the normal events of the past that even I fully realise the incredible changes that have taken place in the coal industry during and since the war. Judging by the frequency of its use 'Britain's peaceful social revolution' appears to be one of those convenient phrases that has been elevated to the statesmanlike level of the politely platitudinous, along with 'democracy' and 'the free world'. When the museum-piece correspondence columns of the *Daily Telegraph* and the inanities of 'Peter Simple' lay claim to the phrase, the coinage is certainly in danger of being debased. But 'revolution' is the one word that can be legitimately used in any discussion on coal-mining and the people that live by it, a revolution made by the combined effects of the war, the Labour Government and the National Coal Board, and most immediately felt by the fortunate people of my generation.

Ten years ago this New Year the NCB flag was hoisted with celebrations and joyful demonstrations at every pit-head in the country. This anniversary has been politely greeted by even those sections of the press that had most consistently opposed the idea of nationalisation. The articles have been almost solely concerned with the economics of the industry, and, if fair, have shown that the Coal Board is engaged in a heavy investment programme, sinking new shafts and modernising equipment in even the smallest mines. Any comprehensive review of the industry will also show that, with less men, the NCB has raised production from 178 million to 210 million tons a year, that our coal is cheaper than any other in Western Europe, and the British miner (whose 'absenteeism' is, I gather often made much of in discussions on his work) has gained a lead in efficiency and effort over his European counterparts. It might also be remembered that the Board has achieved this despite a statutory obligation to avoid a financial loss over a period of years (in an industry that was badly in need of heavy capital investment), continual difficulties in recruiting sufficient manpower, and a dangerous shortage of top-flight managers and administrators.

All of which is very commendable—but to me, and to everyone who is at all intimate with the mining communities, the ten-year anniversary of the NCB should emphasise not only the economic difficulties and achievements, but also the amazing and sweeping changes in morale, habits and outlook that have at long last been achieved. *The Road to Wigan Pier* is now, thank God, a book for the shilling-all-this-shelf, one of the many invaluable social protests held in the floppy mustard covers of the Left Book Club, a piece of *history*.

The miners were undoubtedly the most militant and closely-knit section of the working classes, people who seemed to have the lessons of the past stamped irremovably into their very minds. It is difficult to convey just how this was so without exciting the incredulity of those who do not know the mining areas. I was brought up to regard 'tory' as the dirtiest of all oaths, and the Royal Family as useless, miserable wasters. Sir Winston Churchill is remembered today more as the man who once ordered the troops to South Wales than the great war leader intoning about the beaches. (This is merely reported as a fact, not as a provocative remark. I once made a similar factual observation in the Union, and was surprised to be accused of undue bitterness! It may perhaps be some consolation to know that the day Mr Attlee received his title he joined the legions in the Party who were 'in it for what they could get'.)

The NCB inherited a tremendous capital of initial goodwill, but also a vast heritage of hatred and suspicion, two emotions that had often grown into sheer unreasonableness and were certainly not those most conducive to successful labour relations. There was inevitably much disappointment when the Board had, from necessity, to retain many of the old, discredited administrative personnel and the old system of 'incentives', so great was the national need for coal. Neither would it be truthful to maintain that the relations between the NUM and the NCB were always ideal, or that many resentments were not still being aired: 'The NCB, the servant of the Tory Government and big business, intend to get the last ounce of work out of the miners . . . the plans are for more production, with greater speed and fewer men. At Bedwas we have seventeen men on the list for redundancy at the present moment. Don't forget the Fleck Committee's findings—drive and discipline for the miners. We should stop them NOW.' Thus finishes a letter in a NUM magazine, an attitude which is certainly not widespread, but indicative of the sort of suspicion the NCB has had to overcome. Significantly, the same issue of this magazine contained a list of scholarships for degree courses, post-graduate courses, travel scholarships, etc., available for miners and their dependents, and offered by the NCB.

The nationalised industries often appear merely to have changed their ownership, and made little effort to enter into the life of the community. The National Coal Board is to be congratulated on making a genuine effort to get to terms with the mining communities, and the full scope of its achievements is not often realised or praised. Drive and initiative are all too commonly assumed to be an attribute only of 'capitalism', but the NCB has increased production, carried through tremendous changes and yet kept to a very substantial degree the good-will of the miners.

The morning shift still comes home at twenty-five past three, but not with black faces and steel-tipped boots. Pigeons and whippets are now rare pets; television aerials finger from the roofs; there has been only one fatal accident this year in my father's pit. Admass, of course, has seen to it that some of the changes have actually been for the worse, and I prefer the old whippet to Elvis Presley's 'Hound Dog'. But it is a strange thought that the NCB of all organisations is mostly responsible for the thinly attended and faintly apologetic shuffle still called the 'May Day Demonstration', an unrecognisably anaemic descendent of the long, hungry marches of the thirties.

(*May 22, 1957*)

I am arrogant in my ignorance about the major things we should do because I am still involved in the realisation of the *possibility* of these things, and, on the whole, confident in my criticisms of the existing order. (Brian) Walden, on the other hand, is ignorant in his arrogance, because it is based upon a blindness towards most of the worst faults in our society.

(*May 21, 1959*)

Brian Walden, *television inquisitor and former Labour MP, described Oxford as a turning point in his life. The son of a glazier, he admitted to knowing nothing about the university before he came up. 'When I stepped out of the station at Oxford I asked the porter "Where's the university?"' he said. At Queen's College, Walden, a scholar, used to sit reading in a cold, unheated bedroom with an overcoat on because he did not know he had a living-room with a gas fire as well. As president of the Oxford Union in 1957, he was subject to an inquiry into allegations that he tried to persuade* Isis *editor Potter to publish a piece harmful to an aspiring Presidential candidate.* Isis *'Idol' said, 'Friendship with Walden is, in fact, only possible if the marginal importance of it to him is accepted.'*

Potter and Potterism

Left-wing hagiology is full of men, whose lives were motivated by a mood of protest against existing iniquities. Perversely, mankind retains a keener memory of their actions, rather than their moods, though the former may have stemmed from the latter. Dennis Potter appears to believe that there is something intrinsically commendable about 'the mood of protest' itself, regardless of its consequences. It is true that those

153

purveyors of 'the mood', not in his especial care, sometimes get the odd brickbat; and it is also true that when his paroxysms of dissatisfaction subside somewhat, he is prepared to speak of 'our sterile rather boring anger'. No man should be judged on his footnotes. Potter frequently points out that 'the mood' and its devotees are performing a very valuable service for the Left, and I think his disciples would advance this as the Authorised Version, and forgive his occasional heterodoxy.

Potter has a peculiar ambivalence towards legislation. On the last occasion that I was favoured with an oral formulation of his views, he made it quite clear that 'the mood', being a Good in itself, was under no obligation to spawn anything else. Now Osborne curtly declined to do any 'social sanitary' work, but Potter cannot bring himself to shuffle off all responsibility for action, and his interminable gropings to suggest something constructive, derivative from his flailings, reveal his inner confusion. In the circumstances, it is hardly surprising that he clings to 'the mood'. It is more than a release of frustration; it is Dennis Potter's fig-leaf, decently shrouding any flaws in the argument, serving sometimes as a means for avoiding argument altogether. On those rare days when he crawls out of his cocoon and faces his Labour Party critics, Potter is often forced to admit that much of what he writes and says is contradictory, that many of his facts are wrong, that his knowledge of a particular subject is slight or non-existent, and his diatribes upon it are therefore somewhat less than fair. How does Dennis Potter excuse past errors, and present intent to go on committing future errors, without the slightest attempt to meet points which he has just admitted are valid? 'Well, it's the mood,' he says petulantly, 'you cannot give up the mood.' That is the ultimate invocation; no arguments are allowed to be valid against 'the mood'. This self-induced blindness means that the real fight for a normal man, is for Potter a sham battle. Political organisation bores him, and its needs annoy him. He approaches political discussion, not as a means of seeking facts or developing conceptions with an eye to future action, but as a useful way of defining certain attitudes, expressing psychological frustrations, and seeking temperamental affinities. All this becomes clearer as we look from Frankenstein to the Monster, from Potter to Potterism

154

(the grandmaster's own published utterances). Let us take just one example, his article in the first *Isis* of this term.

Facts and figures are treated with stern irreverence in Potter articles. Where a maleficent society has failed to provide statistics to support a case, the Prophet himself invents them. Thus the 80 per cent. of the working class who vote Labour. Even on the narrowest basis yet devised by psephologists for that nebulous entity—'the working class', no such figure has ever been arrived at. Optimistic estimates put Labour's working-class dominance at 2 to 1, not 4 to 1 as Potter claims. That overturns the only bit of analysis Potter attempts, because the argument based upon the fake statistic is naturally invalid. Potterites will not be unduly discouraged, however, as reasoning has never been Ishmael's forte. It is the emotional fervour which commands respect, and this is not lacking. Indeed, Potterism requires frequent emotive use of the word 'Socialist', as an essential substitute for embarrassing explanations. We ought to have more trust 'in a consistent Socialist ideology'. The Labour Party is the only instrument for bringing into existence 'anything remotely resembling a Socialist society'. The Labour Party has 'traded' away 'a certain amount of traditional Socialist theory'. The Labour party wishes to soft-pedal 'the less popular aspects of Socialism'. Potter supplies no definition of Socialism, nor does any one definition become apparent from the article. Yet all this is written at a time when there are a dozen competing definitions of 'Socialism'. Everybody on the left wants to pin the shining medal of 'Socialism' on the particular policies which are personally favoured. As Potter has told us elsewhere that he has an equal contempt for Old Right, Old Centre, and Old Left, some of the above references are, to say the least, puzzling. Incidentally, at this point occurs a good example of the ethics of Potterism. In the middle of all these undefined references to 'Socialism', the following extract appears:

> 'Mr Gaitskell has only to indulge in a fair splattering of the set phraseology, an occasional reference to "Socialism" . . . and we come to heel.'

Potter puts inverted commas around Gaitskell's Socialism,

though not of course around his own. Dennis Potter must be permitted to use 'Socialism' to fill any gaps in his thought, but he has no intention of allowing anyone else a similar licence.

Much the most cherished principle of Potterism is that one's opponents are never to be allowed to possess any intellectual honesty, or genuine convictions. They must not only be wrong, but also base. We are told that because the leadership knows that it can take Dennis Potter's loyalty for granted (yes, it surprised me too), it has decided to cheat him out of the policies he wants, and substitute other policies in which nobody in the Labour Party believes, so that other people, who do believe in them, can be swindled into voting for the Labour Party. The Annual Conference of the Labour Party approves of and connives at this chicanery of course, and it all goes to show how many crooks there are around and about. Dennis Potter has now defeated this shabby scheme by exposing it, though we must not be too sure that he has actually done us a good turn, because in the next sentence he tells us that the whole dirty deal 'is an understandable and sometimes legitimate one within the framework and momentum of gradualist and democratic Socialism'. This typically Potteresque method of stating the case leaves us in some doubt as to whether, overwhelmed by nausea, he is condemning the transaction, or whether he regards it as a necessary bit of business. What is quite clear, however, is that conviction does not enter into the matter at all. The leaders of the Labour Party, the leaders of the Trade Union movement, and half the rank and file of the party do not believe in most of the policies which they advocate. So now you know why we must have lots of protest, or in this case perhaps not.

Finally the theoretician steps upon the boards, and we are given The Potter Theory of the Party. This is such a rousing call to action, that I will quote it in full for those who were unfortunate enough to miss it:

> 'A radical party should splutter with life and polemic, should excite the intellect and emotions and all the while be satisfied only if it disturbs the complacencies and polite hypocricies that continue to riddle English life and debate.'

A beautiful vision, somewhat spoiled by the fact that no less a person than Dennis Potter himself believes that a Labour Party so conducted will be regularly defeated by the Tories at the polls.

> 'The path to power will perhaps always lie in softening the hard edges of ideas and purpose in a snow of elegant platitude and timid statesmanship.'

The optimists will have noticed the slightly indecisive 'perhaps', and will take heart. The New Party may at some distant date 'splutter' into power, providing this is the idea. It may be that it is actually desired and intended that it should be in permanent opposition. Anyway, it's a fascinating field for speculation, much more entertaining than those 'ambiguous' policy statements. Besides, there is always this consolation about Potterism; it is perfectly suited to all shades of protest and every mood of revolt, because any guess you choose to make about what it means will not be stultified by a rebuttal from the founder, who isn't sure either.

(May 13, 1959)

Alan Coren *won a scholarship at Wadham College where he gained a First in English. It was the only subject where style was as important as content, he later said. He has been editor of* Punch *since 1978. Re-reading his student work, he said, 'They came at me like a sudden gust from an open grave.'*

Tough at the Top

Although I am not strictly *in* the entertainment business, if you look carefully, in the right places, you will see me around with the crowd; and I often appear among the also-rans in the small print at the bottom of write-ups about Variety Club dinners. There is no real reason for me to mix with the neon names, except that I like to be where the grass is growing. And this explains why, on that particular day, I happened to be stationed behind a glass in Ferdi's, enjoying everybody else's rehearsal breaks.

Ferdi's is a typical unprepossessing little drain, situated somewhere under the pavement of Jermyn Street, decorated largely with three or four Names and a big drifting cast of hungry nobodies; it also has mirrors, so that everyone can see everyone else just by lifting one eye over the rim of their glass, without disclosing that they really care who's who. This is how I first noticed Elgin Boon that morning; I saw the yellow suede boots (he has weak ankles) shuffle down the stairs, and then the whole glorious figure appeared through the smoke. He saw me; so he smiled and ambled across to where I was dug in. He is always very pleased to see me, as apart from being a very nice person, I don't want to go on the pictures.

'Hallo, Joe. Good to see you.'

'And very pleasant to see you, Elgin,' I said. 'How is it?'

'Very nicely, thank you.' Elgin is a most polite little man.

'A little fuel?' I asked him.

'Most welcome, Joe.'

For a while we sat there filling in recent history; but all the time I had that feeling of Elgin's talking on one level and thinking on another. Disturbing. So the next time there was a break for nourishment, I let the silence hang around on its own. Finally Elgin said:

'I have a new star I want you to meet, Joe.'

'That's very flattering,' I said. 'I liked the last little girl. The Mecca Ballroom Queen, I think she was.'

'Yeah. She sells soap on television now.' He wagged a finger solemnly. 'But her time will come.'

'With you behind her, she can't fail.'

Elgin smiled graciously. He isn't too big to accept flattery. That's what I like about the Business; the bigger they are, the bigger the heart.

'Who's the new angel?' I asked.

'This one isn't a girl. My specialist says I have blood-pressure. But this one is—is—' he was groping around for a blurb, '—is the harbinger of the new celluloid era.'

'Oh. I must meet him.'

'You can do that right now,' said Elgin.

I naturally looked round for some crew-cut god in an Italian suit, but there was no one waiting in the slips. I turned back to Elgin. 'Where is he?'

The agent's eyes were distant. 'Give us Horror,' he murmured, 'they're crying out to me for Horror; the New Movement in the Film Industry—Dracula, Frankenstein— with their families: Things—big Things, nasty little Things, hairy, blood-sucking Things; Things from beneath the sea, above the clouds, out of the Past, out of the Future—Things from the Christ-Knows-Where. And the audience sits there, hungry for more.' He sighed quietly.

'This I know, Elgin,' I said. 'Is your new boy a Horror-rôler or something?'

'The one to end them all. When he finishes his film, half the country will be sleeping with the lights on.'

Some actor, I thought. 'You must introduce me.'

Elgin Boon smiled. Now I look back, I seem to remember it was rather a terrible smile. Then he fished in his overcoat pocket, and produced a tobacco tin, which he laid carefully on the little table and gently eased open. At first I didn't believe it. Out of the tin, and on to the shining marble, ambled a very large, very black, very hairy spider. Instead of running away, it waited, looking at me and Elgin with its eight beady little eyes. I pushed my chair back. I never got on with spiders somehow; I found one once in the lavatory of a four-star hotel; I stay somewhere else now.

'What,' I said—but quietly and calmly—'is that?'

Mr Boon gazed caressingly at the monster. 'That's my boy!'

'That?' I said.

The Spider threw two or three eyes in my direction. 'Waddya mean, "that"?' it snarled.

Elgin spread out a restraining hand to the Spider. 'Don't work yourself into a sweat, son. He's just surprised, that's all. By the way, this is Joe Turkey.'

'Good ter know ya,' said the Spider.

'Thanks.' I felt uncomfortable. There must be some sort of social code for mixing with insects, but Emily Post doesn't seem to have got around to working it out.

'Joe,' said Elgin earnestly, 'you see before you the manifestation of the change in the Industry. The shift in the Balance of Power. Actors are out. Insects are in.'

'Who's a inseck?' said the Spider indignantly. 'How many times I tole ya about mixing me up wid all them crummy ants 'n' flies? I aint no gnat.'

Elgin blanched. 'Don't lose your temper, son. I apologise.'

I had never seen Elgin acting this way before over a protégé. Usually, he takes no lip. And he could tell what I was thinking: he leaned over and took my sleeve.

'He's very sensitive,' he whispered.

By this time I was feeling a little odd. Which I don't mind saying. I called the waiter across.

'The same, Jack. Very deep.'

There was a little cough from the next table. 'Next time,' said the Spider nastily, 'ask if maybe I'd like a shot.'

I became most acid. 'I'm awfully sorry'—I can be very cold at times—'I didn't realise you drank.'

'So happens I do. See?' He smiled a distinctly spidery smile. 'Among other things.'

I looked at Elgin.

'He takes DDT,' said the agent miserably. 'It'll finish him one day.'

'Drop dead!' growled the Star. 'I kin take it or leave it alone.'

The waiter glided up and lowered his cargo just in time; I had that queasy feeling that my sang wasn't quite as froid as it might have been, especially as nobody else seemed to be taking any notice of Elgin's protégé; they were all loping around in the gloom, looking for shoulders to rub. As the drink smoothed off the rough edges in my stomach, I glanced at the Spider, who was watching about seventeen people at once, and muttered to Elgin:

'He may look good—but can he act?'

Whenever I had said this in the past, it had always sounded sharp and no-nonsense. Now I wasn't so sure.

Elgin just smiled tolerantly.

'A natural. See *The Fly*?'

'No.'

'Shame. Stole the picture. Not only acted the title role right off the screen, he also knocked him off for breakfast when we finished shooting.'

'He's learning a lot about the Business,' I said. I was beginning to have an unwilling respect for the little atrocity. 'Do any acting before?' I asked.

The Spider reflected. 'Coupla crowd scenes. Walk-on in *The Ten Commandments*—with about ninety thousand others; usual caper; you know. Then I got my break. I'm hanging around in The Brown Derby, listening to the chit-chat, when suddenly I heard Selznick yell out 'Waiter! There's a fly in my soup!' So quick as hell I flashes on to his table, before anyone kin move, and hoists this fly out of his lunch and stows it away. Selznick sits there dumb, so I takes my chance to belt out the slop scene from *Waterfront*. For a bit no one says nuttin; until

161

Elgin, who happens to be in Hollywood at the time, and sitting at the next table, sprints across and starts putting me over big. Next thing, word is all over everywhere, and I am testing for *The Fly.*'

Elgin was beaming.

'He tells a good story, eh, Joe?'

'Sure.' I said. But not too enthusiastically, you understand. 'What plans?'

'Start shooting a new one next week. Great story. Horror, plus—and this is where it'll hit 'em—plus *human* interest.' Elgin's misty look drifted back. 'I am going to make the Horror film a work of art, Joe. I am going to make it beautiful. Poetic. In this one, strontium—very topical you'll notice—de-sexes all male human beings; but at the same time it belts up the size and potency of spiders; naturally, to prevent humanity turning in its toes, a compromise has to be arranged. Of course, the women put up a bit of a struggle at first . . .'

'Can't unnerstand it,' murmured the Spider.

'. . . but after the High Priest of the spiders . . .'

'Guess who,' said the Spider modestly.

'. . . after he carries off the Queen of this Swedish Sun-Cult to his web, and she succumbs to his—his Arachnid charms . . .'

'And the rest.'

'. . . after that, society accepts the inevitable answer, and Bingo! we got a happy ending.'

'Happy?' I offered.

'Sure. They breed a race of six-legged, four-eyed Spumans.'

'Spumans?'

'Spumans.'

'Delightful,' I said. 'Enid Blyton must be doing the screenplay.'

The Spider looked at me sharply. '*I'm* doin' the screenplay,' it said.

'Oh. I'll take odds you're a company in six months.'

'I'm woikin' on it.'

I looked at Elgin, but he just grinned limply and said: 'Independent, isn't he?'

I stood up to go. A little hazy. But before I could crawl out from behind the table, a long, rangy figure elbowed his way through the crowd, and, as the record covers say, suddenly it was Phineas Beale! Phineas is Elgin Boon's right-hand man and chief scout; physically he is his complete opposite. Elgin is pink and spherical, Phineas yellow and stringy; if they were a team on the other side of the fence, they would look like gimmick-sellers. As it is, they are the most formidable talent-men on crêpe. Phineas was breathing very heavily, and his long bony arms and legs were jerking about, knocking off glasses, rearranging teeth, and generally clearing a space for some distance around, which in Ferdi's is pretty unusual. And in one fist he was clutching a paper carrier-bag.

'Anchor up, Beale!' snapped Elgin, and the tall figure relaxed like a folding umbrella; he dropped into the chair opposite.

'Elgin!' gasped his lieutenant. 'Elgin, I have in my hands, in my possession, that is, within, in other words, contract distance, I hold, as one might say, the rights, control, and to a certain extent, that is,' Phineas was becoming dim through the flying spray, 'power of attorney for the greatest, most stupendous, most cineramic box-office draw since I don't know when.'

'All right. Surprise me!'

Beale's eyes flicked open. He paused dramatically, and took from the carrier-bag a large glass preserving-jar and placed it reverently on the table. The crowd seethed. I leaned forward. Inside the jar was a particularly repulsive member of the crab family, peering at us with a pair of little metallic eyes. I feel about crabs the same way I feel about spiders. Only more so.

Suddenly, all around us, it was quiet. The moment of truth.

'Well?' said Elgin, guardedly.

Beale breathed, rather than said:

'Our new star!'

Without moving his head, Boon looked up at the other's straining face. 'We have our hands full, Beale. We're pushing the Spider, remember? And what is so special about this thing? Except it's bigger than the Spider.'

The Spider, which up till then had remained silent, decided to assert itself.

'So? Beefcake!' it snorted derisively. 'Ya think this lousy speck of sea food is gonna give *ME* the pusheroo?' And it laughed, as only a spider can laugh.

Phineas Beale replied with one of his large range of diabolical

163

grins. The crowd took its belt in a couple of notches. And a silent question flashed from Boon to Beale, who paused for a long, calculated moment, then reached across to the jar and prised off the lid.

From within there came a rich, throbbing, baritone voice. And it was saying:

'. . . in this petty pace from day to day.
To the last syllable of recorded time;
And all our yesterdays have lighted fools
The way to dusty death. Out, out . . .'

The voice boomed; it rose and fell; it cried; it suffered.

I have never heard Ferdi's so silent. The only background to the Crab's performance was Phineas Beale's satisfied breathing.

'. . . signifying nothing.'

They cheered until the glasses fell off the bar. But the best was yet to be.

Beale lifted a majestic hand for silence. It fell. He took hold of the jar, and laid it carefully on its side. The Crab shook itself, then slowly and deliberately made a sideways entrance on to the table. The two stalk-eyes glinted at the trembling audience.

'And now, friends,' it said in that same mellow tone, 'one or two little items from my extensive repertoire.'

I won't go into details; especially as they're a trifle blurred. In short, the Crab knocked out four items from *The Desert Song*, recited 'East Coker', did an impression of James Stewart, and ended up with a soft-shoe routine from *Broadway Melody*.

The club went mad; columnists were fighting each other to get up the stairs; top-line actors were telling their friends how they were going to open little grocer's shops in East Anglia, away from it all. Elgin and Phineas were sweating over their small black address books. And nobody noticed the Spider. But as the howling mob poured out of the bar, our table went flying under their feet. Half a minute later, Ferdi's was empty, except for me and Jack, the barman. It was Jack who first caught sight of the Spider; it had been trodden into the purple carpet. We knelt down, and saw one leg kicking feebly, and one eye blinking away a tear. A tiny, heartbreaking whisper came out with its last breath:

164

'I could—I coulda been—*some*body.'

Jack shook his head. 'Tough.'

I looked at the stain on the carpet which might have been the first of the Spumans.

'Ah, well,' I said quietly, 'that's Show Business.'

(October 29, 1958)

John Fuller *won the Newdigate Prize in 1960 while still a student at New College. He lives in Oxford and became a fellow of Magdalen College.*

Sciamachy

I

Whoever from the stinking village calls
   One quick accusing word,
   Or stiffens, circling like a bird
About the empty air, or who has heard
Some wall beneath a finger hiss, he falls.

This knowledge is not good. We must invent
   The sparkling education
   Of the Dog, condone the bun
Crammed in its gob: our cure has now begun
A drooling torturer, green, in its tent.

Agents of nothing, drumming, men without size
   Surround the ageless paws
   (We, mirrored, are ourselves the cause)
Accusing of their self-inflicted sores
It! Ha! The web is fragile! Tell no lies!

By violent deaths are we at length outdone:
   In the last substitute act,
   The final wagging of a fact
Slammed down the slowly tilting scales and cracked
The suffering filament, so hardly spun.

The ease of the marvels planted firmly in,
    Birds at their smiling heads
        And little boats
Bobbing nuisances
    At great stone feet:
        It threatens us with murder
            Nicely done
    Under these pious hands.
        Blue moon-faced clocks
(Barbs, fishes, brazen suns
    Like bitten flowers)
        Assault with tinny janglings
            Of the bells
    And click for further gongs.
        The people swarm
In thousands, rubbernecking,
    On the mole,
        Weeping and falling,
            Cut themselves for fun.
    Taking each others' ears,
        Shaking them hard
Until the bits fly out,
    They shout and bleed.
        On springy turfs
            Peppered with rabbit droppings
Squibs explode by sphinxes
    Under porcelain skies.
The Dog unmercifully
    Grins and squints
        At all the bright confusion,
            All the deaths.
    The keys of my machine
        Like horses' hooves
Race with their printed symbols on the page!

(*October 29, 1958*)

The Sixties and After

Auberon Waugh *left Christ Church after a year without taking his degree in Politics, Philosophy and Economics. He described his 1963 novel* Path of Dalliance *as a satire on 'various political, artistic and philosophical excesses at Oxford University from the point of view of an innocent, sexually incompetent undergraduate'.*

A Short Story

She sat absorbed in her reflection across the dressing-table that was also a writing desk, and the gas fire hissed and whispered behind her with a kind of odious, cloying familiarity which sometimes made her think of turning it off. But when she did she found the silence even more oppressive, and she felt alone and rather silly staring at herself in the looking glass without it. She watched her face anxiously for any change and, being unable to find one she started to make whimsical faces, sometimes thoughtful, sometimes as one who finds herself betrayed in love, sometimes as one found in betrayal, sometimes as one who on opening a cupboard door finds the mutilated body of her lover hanging grotesquely from a hook.

Her friends would have been surprised to see her now. In St Agnes' she was thought of as a steady, reliable girl with a mature mind and a sense of responsibility. She sometimes wondered if her friends would take her balanced sensible ideas on contraception and religion quite so seriously if they could see her now, with her bright orange lips contorted in the terrible leer of a mother who has just eaten their baby daughter welcoming her husband back from a hard day's work in the woods. At dinner in Hall they had discussed nuclear disarmament with the soup; strangely enough they had all seemed in favour of it. But, as Fanny pointed out, it was not so much a matter of principle as of expediency. That had been a very good point; one should not stress the ethical side of it so much, or everyone would think one was a crank, the sort of person who wore jeans and a beard and brought the whole Campaign into disrepute. Paul was not one of those silly extremists who wore jeans; he wore sensible green trousers with a zip front. She remembered with a little pang the occasion on which she had stupidly spilt some Coca-Cola on them during the Aldermaston march, and the sweet pride with which he had reassured her: 'It's all right, darling. They're waterproof.'

She tried a new face, with her lips pursed and her tongue slightly extended, but then abandoned it when she found that it reminded her of something faintly improper. Sex was so childish, really. It wasn't that she disapproved of it, or was a prude, or anything like that; especially things like homosexuality and free love, which should be encouraged on the intellectual level at any rate. She was not at all shocked by her friend's affair, and rather envious that Fanny should have been able to find someone who was at the same time a Negro, and a Jew and a Communist Nationalist. She did not know that Negroes were ever Jews, and would have been tempted to disbelieve the whole story if she had not known that Fanny was not the sort of girl to make things up.

After the soup they had sardines on toast, and so naturally they talked about South Africa. After that had been clarified they moved on to the usual St Agnes' lemon curd and cream and discussed Peter Jay. If only sex wasn't quite so childish, she thought, making a wistful face; then she bared her teeth and winked at herself to keep her sense of humour.

There was nothing like that between her and Paul, although she might have allowed herself to exaggerate a little to her friends what had happened that evening when she was resting during a spell in the Aldermaston march, and Paul had lent her his duffle to lie on. The truth about Paul, which now she was alone she could admit to herself, was that he really did not pay enough attention to his personal hygiene. Not that that sort of thing mattered to her, of course. It was Paul's mind that attracted her, as she constantly reminded herself . . . and his daring provocative opinion on almost any subject you cared to mention; but she did sometimes wish that he would take just a little more trouble. *She* kept a little cannister called Keep-Fresh, and once, for a joke, had squirted Fanny with it when she wasn't looking. Fanny had said that she did not mind in the least, and could quite see the funny side of it, but as she might have been blinded if it had got in her eyes, she ought to be a little more careful. It wasn't very funny, and she supposed she ought to have thought of it.

'O Lord,' she thought, 'I wonder why Paul did not even touch me all that night.' She had visions of dozens of little children, all with bright orange lips and green terylene trousers, tumbling over each other and calling her 'Mummy', and then she remembered what she and Paul thought about contraception and recollected herself.

Soon she would have to go to her Discussion Group, but she was feeling too miserable for it just then. She tried to meditate on sensible things; on Comprehensive Schools and apartheid, but all the time her mind kept returning to Paul's shiny zip-front and soon she began to feel terribly alone. She pricked her face savagely, and the ugly white marks mocked her efforts to keep herself from crying. She told herself that she had no reason to be wretched, that it was just self-pity, but for once her balanced, sensible opinions seemed to hold no weight, and for a long time she sat without a sound, staring at herself in wordless misery. The gas-fire continued its complacent, confidential whisper, and after a time, without thinking what she was doing but with a kind of greedy haste she crawled towards it, as her only friend, over the cocoa-stained black rug in front of the fire.

(*May 4, 1960*)

Richard Ingrams *went to University College with Shrewsbury schoolfriend Paul Foot, and both wrote for* Isis. *He gained a Third in Classical Greats and became editor of* Private Eye, *successor to the Oxford magazine* Parson's Pleasure. *In 1967, because of a liver complaint, Ingrams gave up drinking entirely. He later said the worst thing about being on the wagon was 'having to listen to people talking nonsense at drinks or dinner parties.'*

William Rushton *was also at school with Ingrams and Foot. Though not a student at Oxford, he drew cartoons for* Isis. *With Christopher Brooker, he helped set up* Private Eye.

Pubs

Many will have noticed the increasing number of advertisements which at first sight do not look like advertisements at all. The latest of these to appear features the legend 'Let's all meet at the pub' and displays a picture of gay suburban people quaffing light ale in an unnaturally jolly bar with smart shiny furniture.

At first sight the injunction seems unnecessary—as if a hoarding were to say 'Let's all go for a walk' and show pictures

171

of large hearty men striding out over the heather. But no! This poster is sponsored by some vast amorphous organisation of brewers who control beer and they are worried by the lack of interest shown by the public. Hence the riotous goings on in Ruislip which the poster portrays.

Now, we have always thought of the British as a beer-drinking nation and our conception of England includes the conception of innumerable pubs, all with fine historic names, in which men in cloth caps down countless pints of beer while they discuss fishing, politics and other relaxing topics. The appearance of the poster suggests that these men no longer frequent the pubs but stay at home knitting or watching the television. We hear the red-faced landlord bemoan 'It's that thar telley wot's done it. Things 'aven't been the same since that started', implying that he is not to blame; it is the new affluent Britishers who by losing interest in their national drink, have caused the pub slump.

There may be something in this, but I prefer to think that the opposite is the case and that the landlord is to blame—that it is he who has changed; that the man who was previously red-faced and jovial, who wore braces and rolled his sleeves up, is now a dapper little man in a suit with smarmy hair and a clip-on bow tie. Similarly his bar, once suited to drinking, darts playing and even singing, is now wall-papererd, carpeted and adorned with artificial flowers. Once a bar; now a teashop. Not only are your eyes assaulted by the clashing colours of magenta wallpaper and bogus tulips, the ears are in many cases jarred by the insidious device of musack, gushing like stale Babycham from loudspeakers on the walls. No wonder the men in cloth caps have hopped it. Any man who can drink beer and listen to Mantovani at the same time without being overcome by a profound melancholy, 'is fit for treasons, stratagems and spoils'. No. I am never merry when I hear sweet (and sickly) musack.

We seldom become sensible to the beauty of buildings, be it churches or pubs, while they are still capable of redemption. No doubt in a few years' time societies will be formed for the preservation of pubs, but by then it will be too late. Perhaps we should accept the change with resignation. But then let the words of Hilaire Belloc be shouted at mine bow-tied, Brylcreemed host and for a moment let the sound of musack be dimmed:

'When you have lost your inns, drown your empty selves, for you will have lost the last of England.'

(*January 25, 1961*)

There is nothing like

a pint of strong ale

to put you

right back on your feet!

The Pub Crawl

The Duke

Terry Jones *has been writing and performing comedy since his Oxford days. He is best known as one of the* Monty Python *team, but recently revealed a second career as a medievalist with the publication of a provocative study of Chaucer's Knight.*

A Short Love Story

She was bent over a basin washing her hair, standing there with the failing light just catching on her shoulders. I knew then that this would be the last time I should be close to her, and the last opportunity I would have to make her hear me. So I called softly:
    'Ada',
for I had known her name from the very first, when I had seen her across that little school-room under the hills; I had said her name to myself no louder than any small boy would dare, not able to brave the jeers and catcalls of the others:
    'Jan loves Ada.'
    So I had sat small and pale in the big class-room that was painted half cream and half chocolate and is dim and dusty now and has no glass in its windows; and I did not tell a soul what I had seen across the desks, that I had sat and watched the new girl all morning and that I did not dare speak to her. In the play-time after lunch, I had walked about the group that collects around any new-comer to the school and that encour-

ages and taunts and giggles, and I had thought that if I had gone up to her and taken her hand, somehow or other she would have recognised me.

'Come on, Jan, and meet the new girl, her name's Ada!' But I would not. As I walked about it and about, I could catch glimpses of her eyes darting around her or glistening when she laughed with the others, and I had felt that there was some sort of commitment between us, and that she would recognise me. But I was afraid, and so I never knew.

But now, as I watched in that kitchen, it was not fear that I felt, so much as anxiety lest I let this final opportunity slip away from me like all the others. For I knew that it was up to me to make the first move. I had to speak out or we should remain just as we always had been.

She would never have spoken to me first, I suppose I had always known that, and that is why we had remained apart and waiting for the time when we should recognise each other in a pushing crowd in Piccadilly Tube Station, years later and for a moment her eyes would glisten, and I should open my mouth but not make a sound, and the crowd would heave and push and pull us apart into the shouldering mass, and I would stagger back, yielding, yet I would feel certain that she too had felt the anticipation and the moment of meeting. But I could not know.

And I remember the weeks after that of self-torture and accusation at the frustration: to have been for one moment at the point of recognition and to lose it and to still be as apart as ever. So this time I called very softly, so as not to frighten her, but also with as much command as I knew how, with my voice low and insistent:

'Ada, Ada.'

In the sun setting, and the small kitchen growing dark, and the water flashing in the bowl, and glittering over her hair, and the smooth shadows on her back moving quietly but strong and lithe. Was that not how she had always been herself? Strong, independent—no, more than independent—somehow cut-off, flitting about in the shadows at the very edges of my existence, but yet somehow essential to its core.

And now, I remember my mother. Yes, I tell you, I remember her whom I never saw alive but once, when I was too shocked by the suddenness of my own being to notice her who died in giving it me. A thin, pale woman sitting at the corner of the fireplace which has now no fire in the grate, sitting in the shadows, still and strong, until a footstep suddenly pricks her to life and, lithe as an autumn fox, her eyes glistening with anticipation in the firelight, she springs to the door and stands waiting behind it, shaking with excitement; but the footsteps in the corridor hesitate outside the door, and then turn away and fade out of hearing. She is my mother, in my imagination, the little old woman in grey, whose face I cannot see and whose shoulders drop with the disappointment, and who turns back to the dying fire and pokes the last embers with a sigh and accepts the interminable separation.

And now: Ada, her face turned away from me, pale and grey in the failing light, working her fingers through her hair as silently and as lonely as I had sat in that big classroom or my mother waiting by the fire for the door which never opened. And myself wanting to yell out to her in my impatience, to burst open the door behind which I had always believed she waited and trembled with anticipation and which separated us; but one fear stops me: lest this belief which I have kept close all through my life be mistaken—a mere fabrication of my own imagination. Lest all those times, in the empty class-room, in the stifling tube-train, and now, in the silence of this dim kitchen, with the green and white squared tiles around the sink and the laved woodwork, where the soap has worn away the paint, and just the stirring of the coke settling in the boiler and the wash of the water against the enamelled basin, lest all these times there has been no potential communication—no commitment at all. Lest she has never realised the separation.

And yet I had to know, now, for certain, had to take this final opportunity to reach over to her, to make her turn round and once and for all admit that she recognised me while communication might still be possible, before her shoulders no longer glistened in the dropping sun, before the night turned cold. I called:

'Ada! my love!' I cried, tears in my eyes, perhaps even on my cheeks; 'Ada! See I am here! I am come at last! my love, my Sun, my Spirit!'

And the light fell from her shoulders as she raised her head and pushed back her streaming hair, water runnelling about her tight-shut eyes and into the cracks:

'Huh! You old fool! Come and help me dry . . . get a bit of beer in you, and you're more like a pimp than a husband!' and I smiled with her and she opened her eyes, but, of course, they were dull and dark.

(January 23, 1963)

Miles Kington *claims he is the son of a famous composer but was abandoned at birth and brought up by gypsies. The creator of the language of Franglais, he studied French and German at Oxford. On leaving he became jazz reviewer for* The Times, *where he now has a daily humorous column. He plays double-bass for the group Instant Sunshine and writes for* Punch.

Upward Glory

Phil D. Kroesus was looking worried. He hadn't looked worried for thirty-five years—he was paid 40,000 dollars a year not to look worried. If his closest friends could have seen him sitting there looking worried, they would have known something was wrong. But the only person who could see him was his secretary, peering at her typewriter through large, blinking spectacles. He didn't have any close friends anyway. He wasn't paid 40,000 dollars a year to have close friends.

He was paid to be President at Kigarette Filters, one of America's largest tobacco concerns. Like many another mythological figure, he had started with nothing to call his own, except maybe his father, who had been President of Kigarette Filters before him. In the intervening years Kroesus had seen other tobacco dynasties burn to their end and smoulder out. They had a saying in the company, what Kroesus didn't know about tobacco wouldn't give cancer to a flea. When long cigarettes had been in fashion, it was Kigarette who had flooded the market with Kingarette—the cigar-length cigarette with the all-tobacco filter. Then when other companies were losing ground to an influx of shorter, more manoeuvrable European models, Phil Kroesus had been the first to produce an American answer—the Amerikigarette, with no filter, no flavour, and only half the length of the European cigarettes. And when the public had tired of short cigarettes, Kroesus had led the way with Kigs, the cigarette which any American father could safely take back to his family.

Phil Kroesus spat with perfect aim and wondered absent-mindedly why no one had ever tried to market Kuspittoons. But somebody must have, some place. There was nothing new. Except this, he thought glumly, and looked at his desk again.

On it lay two documents. One was from the agency that handled their advertising. Most of what it said he knew already. For the last year Kigarette Filters had steadily been increasing their expenditure on television advertising to keep pace with their three or four great rivals. Every time the other companies bought new programmes, he followed them. Every time it turned out that Kigarette Filters was interested in another facet of American culture as seen on television, it turned out that the others were too.

Last month had been the biggest increase of the year for the tobacco industry. More and more smiling men appeared on the screen every night and poured their smooth, persuasive words down the American gullet, asking the public to help their cigarettes sell by going out to buy them. Sometimes they supplied reasons, but mostly they just told them to go out and buy. And now, according to this document, somebody in the agency had goofed and forgotten to send in the order for the Kigarette Filters television time. During the last month no advertisement for Kigarette, the cigarette smoked by more anti-Communists than any other brand, had appeared on television.

The other document from Sales Research was much smaller and to the point. It proved conclusively that during the last month their sales figures had not stopped their upward trend.

Phil D. Kroesus was looking worried. Nothing in his experience had prepared him for anything like this. If the sales had gone down, he would have known what to do—shrug his shoulders and switch to another agency. This was different; it was a betrayal of all he had ever worked for. It shook his faith in what he affectionately thought of as the incorruptible imbecility of the American public. Was that what he meant? What he wanted to say was that business had always worked and played on the assumption that demands were created and *then* supplied, and that to content oneself with supplying a demand was like waiting to be proposed to by a woman. That wasn't what he means either, decided Kroesus, thinking of his wife. There were the facts anyway; they had stopped their TV advertising and it had not affected their sales. Now he had to make a big decision.

He looked up and said, 'Miss French!' The typewriter choked on a bullet and stopped firing.

'Yes, P.D.?' said his secretary. He liked to be called P.D. It gave the impression of intimacy and effectively prevented any use of his first name.

'If you did something you hadn't meant to and it worked out OK, would you do it again?'

'I'd do it again,' said Miss French, right on cue.

Kroesus made a big decision and reached for the phone.

'Is that the agency? Kroesus here. Fine thanks. Listen—I want you to pull all our ads out of television, radio and newspapers. Take down all our billboards. I don't want to see Kigarette Filters advertised anywhere for the next month. Yes, I'm fine thanks. And for the next month I am also unavailable.'

Four weeks later, at a shareholders' meeting, Kroesus gloomily admitted to those present that sales had now risen 15 per cent in the last two months and showed no signs of halting their disastrous course. He had no choice in the circumstances but to double all dividends and hoped that they would sympathise with him in his position. They all rose spontaneously as he left the room and more than one person had to choke back a tear.

In his office, Kroesus reviewed the disunited state of his mind. He found civil war going on there. One half said that people had always been slaves to the old kind of advertising, the other half argued that if the slaves were liberated, they could afford to buy more cigarettes. That is to say more

Kigarettes. He was reassured by this last, but was still worried by the thought of abandoning advertising. The agency had sent him a friendly note to remind him that in America more was spent on advertising than on defence, that advertising going out of fashion means a recession, recession meant poverty, and poverty meant only one thing—less Kigarettes would get smoked. He could see no way out of this problem.

'Miss French!' The typewriter hurried through a florid cadenza and fell silent.

'If you had made a new discovery which didn't fit in with advertising what would you do?'

'Make advertising fit in with it?'

He thought for a bit till he saw what she meant, and picked up the phone.

Three weeks later vast posters appeared all over the country showing, in stark white lettering on a black background the words THE CIGARETTE THAT NEEDS NO ADVERTISING. No name, just a message. Television viewers were faced one night with a thirty second advertisement showing a man sitting at a table smoking a cigarette for thirty seconds. No hidden voice, no writing. No expression on the man's face—or was there a slight smile? Kigarettes were displayed in shops in plain white packs with no inscription except Filter and Non-Filter.

Kigarette Filter sales had now risen a total of 25 per cent in three months. Other tobacco companies had noticed these strange new practices in the industry and were alarmed. Himalayan Tobacco Inc. (makers of Rockies, the menthol cigarette with the subtle taste of tobacco) secretly put out posters on the same lines and found that the public assumed they were Kigarette advertisements. As Kigarette sales went up, theirs went down. The American public wasn't smoking any more, it was just smoking more Kigarettes. And their secret, no longer a secret, could by its very nature be used only by the person who thought of it first.

American democracy and American advertising were closely connected in Kroesus's mind. For him, the Statue of Liberty was the greatest brand image in the world. Although he was not outwardly an emotional man, he loved his cigarette-smoking country and dreaded to think that there was perhaps something wrong in what he was doing. The way things were going, he was heading for a monopoly, and monopolies were undemocratic, unless held by the government. Or was that socialism? He felt confused.

'Miss French!' They typewriter stalled in mid-air.

'Do you believe in free competition?'

'And is the logical conclusion of free competition trying to force your rivals out of business?'

'So it seems to me.'

His face cleared. He was backed by unbiased opinion. Before he knew it, he was asking to be put through to the agency.

They redesigned to his orders an old poster which had read—'Kigarette—the only cigarette which combines good taste with a good taste'. America got up one morning and was faced with the uncompromising message 'The Only Cigarette'. No one doubted which one was meant and it made them feel good to know it.

When Kroesus opened his afternoon mail that day, he found that the two great political parties had written to him. They both hailed him as an outstanding example of their organisation and both pointed out that although the present President was in many ways a fine man, he did not fully represent the cigarette-smoking majority. At some time convenient to Kroesus, they would be very pleased to make his acquaintance.

Kroesus looked worried. Nothing in his experience had prepared him for anything like this.

'Miss French!'

(March 13, 1963)

A Complete Victorian Novel

The three of them presented a quaint spectacle as they walked through the municipal park of D*****, in the year 18**, with the dog R***** playing round their f***.

—Mr Jellicoe and I are two of the biggest treacle manufacturers in the country, claimed fat, jolly Mr Carlisle, swinging at a dandelion with his number five umbrella. To young Tom, certainly, he seemed a giant.

—For your interest, young man, I stand six foot five in my

stockinged feet, boomed Mr Jellicoe.

—A habit I am trying to break him of, added Mr Carlisle.

—With no success, subtracted Mr Jellicoe.

It was spring in the park (the rest of the town lay in permanent industrial winter). On Tom's left strode Mr Carlisle, his face dumpling when he smiled, and on his right, Mr Jellicoe, his Gothic face neatly divided in half by a noble nose.

—Now, Tom. Your mother, who is my deceased brother's wife, has asked me to look after you until such time as you can look after her. I will apprentice you to the treacle trade; in four years' time you can earn your fare to London where you will cultivate the conversation of the great, write an astounding novel and return here penniless.

Tom looked up questioningly into Mr Carlisle's face. Jellicoe took over confirmatively.

—We've seen it happen before. Your uncle keeps in the office a rejected manuscript of his, entitled, How Jemima broke her word to her father and was saved by the timely intervention of a disguised gentlemen with a title in weekly parts. It helps to while away the occasional slump in the treacle business.

At this moment a barouche swept past them, but not so rapidly that Tom failed to notice the vision of heavenly beauty that sat therein beneath a parasol.

—Who was that? breathed Tom.

—Colonel Wilkinson's daughter, replied his uncle. In due course you will meet her at a ball, lose sight of her for several years, then find her again and discover you have meanwhile become a man.

—On the other hand, said Mr Jellicoe, the lucky girl may be Isabel Crosby, Sir Edward's daughter, who is at present in the south of England, pining for her native moors and rough stone walls.

—Meanwhile, Tom, let us hie us to the factory where I shall show you the high stool and dusty ledger with which you will share the next four dreary years.

—And introduce you to Ephraim Stackley, who will sit next to you reading highly unrealistic novels all day, which will, however, strike poetry in your soul and inspire you to deeds of which poor faithful Ephraim is quite incapable.

Young Tom was quite confused by all this, but managed to stammer, When I am rich, uncle, I will come back and share my wealth with you and Mr Jellicoe.

—That, said Mr Carlisle, rubbing his hands together, is very intelligent of you, Tom. And now, if you don't mind, I shall give you a brief insight into the history of molasses.

(May 9, 1964)

Gyles Brandreth *was admired in the Oxford Union for commanding attention during a debate by performing a headstand on the President's chair, and well launched by the time he left the university. He remains a prolific writer and broadcaster with a penchant for discovering unusual games.*

The Breast

The breast is in. Discretion once kept her hidden, but today she is everyone's idol. You are not just treated to the breast solus: you pays your money and you takes your choice, for the moving picture playhouses now throw them at you in pairs: pinkened avocadoes, tinged with ruby goose-pimples. It is a sight to quicken the eyebrows of any man, as he sits in the three-and-nines, his clammy paw fumbling in the bag of jujubes.

Soon, no doubt, the saucy camera will saunter to the nether regions. But when it has, when Julie Andrews has revealed her sumptuous all, that will be that. Woman (bless her fluffy heart) does not amount to much, so as soon as we've seen it once we'll have seen it all. Sloppy, pansyatic, socialist elements, still want to give her a boost, but history has shown (for history does this sort of useful thing) that woman—for all her breasts and breeding—is not quite up to it.

Around the world, spotty, dandruff-ridden youths are

fumbling down darkened alleys and bright halls in search of a fruity wench—not just for a quaint heaveho among the gardenias, but for a lifelong companion, colleague and friend. What does he find?

If you think I jest and jape, ask yourself (or selves—it is an increasing problem) who are the women who enrich this peanut of a world. Think for a moment, and all you'll come up with is Babs Castle, Katie Boyle and Danny la Rue.

Yes, it is distressing. The breast, of course, is the glorious consolation. A woman may be dauntingly mature, purple about the face, quivering about the lips and chins—yet still raise a smile or a laugh or even the occasional nostalgic sigh, as she exposes in that perpetually innocent but candid manner— oh, how they can be innocent and candid these days!—the plump arena of crumpled flesh. She may be an unsuccessful second viola in life's tea-time band, a washed-out drudge in the kitchens of the world, a creamy intellectual sporting her virginity on her sleeve for daws to poke at, an obsessive breeder whose role is as humdrum and haphazard as that excellent little 1893 Chekhov story—but still she asks, plaintively though silently (she is such a paradox), she asks us to forgive all that. And out it comes, like a faithful bassett-hound sniffing the undergrowth on Hampstead Heath, taunting, teasing, playful, the hot cross bun of man's desiring: the left breast.

Give me a left breast and I am your man, embittered, self-confessed, heady with dreams Olympus high, a sort of decadent Peter Pan, a slobbering candidate for Nipples Anonymous.

(October 25, 1967)

Maggie Gee's *first novel,* Dying In Other Words, *was written while still in her twenties and published in 1981.*

Bath Night in Somerville
Gowns will be worn

Only the callowest of males (who can heartily hoof it along the path to the bath in mockery-proof muscular nudity), could claim that scholarships don't count. The Girls' Bath Gang, a cold-blooded and persecuted minority, know different. The nakedness of woman is the work of God, but one more aberration might lead the Orthodox Abstainers to plug-stealing direct action.

Naked democracy doesn't work unless all the baths do. It has to be a case of Scholars and Oarswomen first. Oarswomen of course, are a quite different kettle of duckweed, sweat and once a rumoured fish . . . even the Senior Scholar, a theologian, once remarked, wistfully flexing her apocryphal biceps, that perhaps tracksuits took talc better. (But for most of us, lacking the essential Oarswoman's fresh-from-the-Isis Aura, gowns will be worn.)

We tried to spice the hamline scene with a few maxis, but the SCR refused our invitation to a formal Bath-in. The Chancellor accepted, but the Porter had to be mean about All Gentlemen Out by whatever the invitation said was peak Foaming Fun Time.

The aesthete with her joss-stick scented bath cubes and the zoologist with a furtive rubber duck queue happily together, the Bubble Bath Splinter Group, on every eye an anticipatory rainbow-coloured film, sit a little apart. The Gang's eccentric, tellingly dubbed 'The Nightly', is apparently gazing dully on the ground: in fact she is bitterly counting feet. After the first fine fresher's influx, the Club dwindles into Spring. Still, a hard core will sweat it out till Summer when all but the Nightly will sag into apathy and antiperspirant. The Nightly is bitter. Seven feet, and one of these Athlete's, is bad even for a Thursday.

But when all is quiet the bathsong of the smallest commoner (a new initiate of the Giggle-and-Brag Virgins' Club), floats beatifically into the night above the full-throated hiccups of the plug-hole:

'Oh! We giggle and brag, and we brag and we giggle.

And we're all for a spot of slap and tickle . . .'

Three years of suffering long gowns, emolument-bought loofahs and the Third on the transistor to take precedence over Commoner's cold, a common flannel and Radio Caroline will take their toll.

(February 28, 1968)

Hermione Lee *became a lecturer in English at York University, and a critic. She is author of* The Novels of Virginia Woolf, *a television hostess and a regular reviewer in* The Observer.

Madonna of the Bod

Nine a.m. At this time some of us are cooking scrambled eggs for sleepers; some of us who found bed three hours since have mingled eye-shadow with pillows and are right out till twelve; some of us are gobbling college brek, with little chirps and grins. But this week's lady is slipping quietly but firmly through the doors of the Bod for the day's mystery. Ice-cold schedules reared around her as she left her temple; all will be fulfilled to the letter. She smiles to herself as she walks, a pale and puzzling look: the smile of a disciplined soul. Where she passes, groups converge and whisper, gazing surreptitiously from the windows of the K.A., or brought to a sudden halt at the entrance to Blackwell's: 'Look,' they say in hasty murmurs, 'she's going to get a . . .' And down go the red cloaks on all sides. She passes on aware. How has she achieved this mastery over the weaker urges for respite and human companionship? She stops to speak to a friend. That quiet voice. Those quiet hands. There is something about her.

FRIEND: There is something about you. Gosh.

OUR LADY: [*deprecates*]

FRIEND: Are you working really tremendously hard now I suppose?

OUR LADY: [*deprecates smilingly*]

FRIEND [*enraged and frustrated*]: No, but are you?

OUR LADY [*with mystery*]: Well, no. Well, no.

FRIEND [*subtle*]: Then what about the flicks tonight?

OUR LADY: Well, no. [*smiles*] But thanks.

FRIEND [*sinister, gritty*]: Be at the demo?

OUR LADY [*regretfully*]: I haven't the time. I haven't the time. Don't think me uncommitted [*smiles*] but I haven't time for that just at the moment.

FRIEND [*bouncing ruthlessly*]: Then you must be working really hard then. Gosh.

OUR LADY: Well [*gently*] let's just say that I've got [*pauses*] priorities [*smiles*] at the moment.

FRIEND [*desperate*]: Are you going to get a—

OUR LADY [*quiet, but firm*]: Oh, heavens. I've no idea.

She passes on with that imperturbable glow.

Friend: pass on too in the other direction, and murmur as you go: chiz chiz.

(November 13, 1968)

James Fenton *is remembered by contemporaries for creating a minor fashion at Oxford by dressing in scruffy, threadbare clothes. A journalist, his collected poetry was published in 1982. He said in an* Isis *interview, 'I see poetry as an accompaniment to my life, not as a career.'*

The Frog

A frog hunts on land by vision. He escapes
Enemies mainly by seeing them. His eyes
Do not move, as do ours, to follow prey,
Attend suspicious events, or search
For things of interest. If his body changes
Its position with respect to gravity or the whole
Visual world is rotated around him
Then he shows compensatory eye-movements. These

Movements enter his hunting and evading
Habits only, e.g. as he sits
On a rocking lily pad. Thus his eyes
Are actively stabilized. The frog does not seem
To see, or at any rate is not concerned with
The detail of the stationary world around him.
He will starve to death surrounded by food
If it is not moving. His choice of food

Is determined only by size and movement.
He will leap to capture any object the size
Of an insect or worm provided if it moves
Like one. He can be fooled easily not only
By a piece of dangling meat but by any
Small moving object. His sex life
Is conducted by sound and touch. His choice
Of paths in escaping enemies does not

Seem to be governed by anything more devious
Than leaping to where it is darker. Since
He is equally at home on water and on land,
Why should it matter where he lights
After jumping, or what particular direction
He takes? He does remember a moving
Thing provided it stays within
His field of vision and he is not distracted.

(May 28, 1969)

Libby Purves *was an undergraduate at St Anne's College and later presented Radio Oxford's breakfast programme. While at the university, she helped edit an anthology of work by young poets. She is now a journalist and broadcaster, and writes regularly for* Punch.

Sop the Diarrhoea

Once I wrote rather horrifyingly bad adolescent poetry about uncomprehending lighthouses and Lethean shades. On one occasion I used the iambic pentameter to invite a young man (now employed in the Ministry of Agriculture and Fisheries) to Plumb my Weeping Eyes of Dying Green. But that muse died of self-abuse, and for the last six months I have composed only letters with the unvarying, pure prose opening:

> 'I am co-editing a book of the work of poets under 25 for Sidgwick and Jackson, and having come across your work in *Isis* (Red Mole/Aberystwyth College of Librarianship Magazine/Philip Goatchandler's digs/Balliol Wall, etc.), I would be grateful . . .'

Both editors have had a good deal to be grateful for. Deskfuls of poetry handwritten, typed, clean and obscene, flippant, disturbing and occasionally religious, have resulted from these pedestrian invitations; only in very few cases has a poet's modesty made further coaxing letters necessary. On the advice of our professional colleague, we did not advertise; instead I ploughed through half a bushel of school and university magazines, dropped heavy hints at parties, remembered past acquaintances declaiming drunk in taxis, and begged all new contributors to betray their inspired friends to us. Sally went into a trance and emerged with sackfuls of rather tidy bards who remembered to send s.a.e.'s for return, and typed determinedly on one side of the paper only. There came a point in my summer holiday when I had to hide from the post-master—a genially inquisitive Irish postmaster—who thought I was receiving obscene magazines through the holy post.

He wasn't always far wrong. Before I was asked to collect this anthology, I had not been much concerned with the existence of unprinted poets, and entirely ignorant of the devious mental processes of sexuo-socially Committed Sweat 'n Viet lyrists. I rapidly became obsessed with the idea that 95 per cent of English-speaking literati under twenty-five spent their lives rushing from abortion clinic to gas chamber, panting. Throughout the autumn reading, loins throbbed, jagged wounds howled, flowers Felt the Auric Finger of Decay, and one man asked his beloved to come running like a limp butterfly. A request to Jesus to spit at the windowpane vied in graphic suggestiveness with a fervidly-expressed desire to be enveloped in a moist flap of a girl's lip, and a resolution to Sop the Diarrhoea of Loss. It was not always easy to distinguish between a real liking for a new poem and a sense of pure gratitude at its lack of startling anatomical confessions and ferocious pessimism. And, with apologies to James Joyce and friends, if you write 'womb-wet' in one word, it just looks like Wombat, and that is that.

On the whole, sadly, it seems to be better to be word-drunk than incoherently sincere. As in Cold Comfort Farm, where Elfine's poetry, 'Though technically weak, betrayed a nice nature', some of our eventually rejected poets were obviously of great character. But sometimes subject and expression matched, and we had found another poet; and then the problem lay, pleasantly, in selection. Could we afford to ditch John Whitworth's

> *'Yoghourt wrapped in a skein of silk*
> *And crystal cups of the top of the milk',*

even in the interests of including his

> *'Toad romantic,*
> *Corybantic,*
> *Flaunting in the neon glow,*
> *Jaunting with Jurassic toe'?*

Could we print *all* of Teresa McLean's strange epic on a

> *'Perfect Artist . . . dreaming*
> *Of a medieval castle in his paintbrush?'*

And would Chris Reid's epigram on Obadiah Pinstripe (The inventor of the Pin Stripe Suit) really belong in the same volume as Pacey's 'Lakeland Sequence' or, for that matter, Nick Alexander's essay on pederasty? On the whole, we used six or seven poems at least by each contributor, trying to show the work of individual young poets rather than to make any point about the sort of poetry younger people write. So this is not going to be in any way a representative anthology; the age limit is merely a rough guide, and leads to prove no point about the poets under twenty-five, except that they exist.

A few of our contributors are from Oxford; several are working; two are at school, one works for Senator Muskie, one for the British Council in Algiers; one is in prison for trying to burn down the Imperial War Museum. Our great ambition now is to have a party to which they will all come. Like limp but throbbing butterflies.

(February 27, 1971)

197

Tina Brown's article on London gossip is reputed to have impressed Auberon Waugh and his friends so much that they helped her find work in journalism when she left Oxford. On leaving, she held a party on the river with her Isis *editor Sally Emerson to celebrate their contracts with national magazines. She was editor of* Tatler *until 1983.*

Devil May Care

Naturally I arrive too early. The barman, a grotesque, leering individual called Norman, gives me a three minute eyeball.

'The *Private Eye* lunch?' I ask, nervously.

'You invited?' A knowing smile spreads across his face. 'You're too early.' He indicates a winding staircase behind the bar. 'In fact you're the first to arrive.'

'Who else is coming?'

He leans across the bar and invites me into his confidence. 'Mum's the word,' he whispers hoarsely. 'That's one of my advantages—I have a habit of forgetting names.' He winks conspiratorially; 'Whose guest are you? Ingrams? Marnham? or', he gives it all he's got, 'WAUGH?'

'Mr Waugh,' I reply faintly and retreat into a corner.

The door opens and a jovial, owlish-looking man sidles in. 'Hello,' he says to me. 'Can I buy you a drink? I'm for the *Eye* lunch as well. My name's Wichard Cwossman.' 'What do you do?' I ask, because I never read a newspaper.

'No,' he says, patiently repeating himself in the loud clear voice one normally reserves for Spanish waiters. 'Wichard Cwossman.'

We are interrupted by the arrival of the *Eye* staff. Ingrams, too intelligent one feels for his own peace of mind, casts watchful blue eyes over the room. An Austrian banker whose name no one seems to know, Nigel Dempster (alias Lord Grovel), William Shawcross of the *Sunday Times*, Patrick Marnham who writes the colour section of the *Eye*, Alan Watkins, the mellifluous political editor of the *New Statesman*, and sinister Martin Thomkinson, responsible for the political exposés on the back pages of the *Eye*. We are all present and correct except for Waugh, who is late. We follow the editor, Indian file, upstairs for lunch.

Unlike the pomp and ceremony of the *Punch* gatherings on Fridays, the watchword of the *Eye* lunches is Flair and devil may care. If it resembles any social occasion at all it is probably the Hell Fire Club in the era of John Wilkes—for in every pair of eyes there is a satirical gleam that bodes ill for Wichard Cwossman. The door opens and Auberon Waugh arrives dressed in a pin-stripe suit and ground-length navy blue overcoat.

'The most wonderful thing has happened,' he hisses in an ecstatic whisper. 'Ingrams has invited some Austrian bore and apparently has just discovered that he and Crossbum have shared a wife.'

'My God, where can it have possibly happened,' wonders Shawcross. 'Somewhere in mid Europe at the turn of the century?' The room is small and suitably shabby, a long table is set for lunch in the centre. At the head Ingrams presides, unassertive but firmly in control. I sit between Crossbum and Thomkinson, opposite Auberon Waugh and Watkins. 'I can give you a corruption story for any town in England,' breathes Thomkinson in honeyed tones. At the far end of the table sits the younger contingent, Shawcross, wild-haired and whimsical, Dempster, dapper and ebullient, and at the end Marnham, quieter than the others but with eyes that sparkle with wicked journalistic appraisal.

Norman trudges round with an expression of doom on his

face, impartially doling out melon. 'Sorry sir,' he says apologetically as he drops it over Watkins's suit.

'That's all right, Norman,' says Watkins, whom Waugh has already assured me is 'pure gold'. 'I'll save it and eat it cold in the morning.'

Over lunch Crossbum is made to sing for his supper and his performance is admirable. He has the jovial garrulity and air of witty indiscretion that shows he intends to give nothing away. Occasionally he puts the boot in for a colleague with the obvious intention of the *Eye* taking it up as scandal. Any suggestion from the indefatigable Thomkinson that a politician may be corrupt is dismissed with consummate guile. 'Yes, of course, X is a rogue but an enormously likeable rogue and I will help all I can.'

Ingrams rises from his chair at moments of particular indiscretion and closes the door. Though fairly voluble himself, he prefers the role of listener, knitting beside the guillotine allowing Thomkinson to cross examine with unremitting accuracy and Waugh to provide the air of hilarity with his disrespectful outrages.

The conversation shifts, to the publication of Political Diaries. Apparently Crossman keeps one regularly. 'How much are you getting for yours?' Ingrams asks. '£30,000,' replies Crossman triumphantly. 'From *The Observer*,' (or as Auberon Waugh insists upon calling it, 'Astor's Naughty Knickers Magazine').

'Are you wildly indiscreet about old smoothy-chops' sex life?' asks Waugh.

'Certainly not!' exclaims Crossman stoutly.

'And you're still getting £30,000?'

We are on the second course by now, steak and chips dropped by Norman from a height of ten feet. The following night it is the Diamond Jubilee party of the *New Statesman*. 'How clever of you to hold your party on election day,' says Waugh to Watkins. 'It means you won't have any politicians there. Not even awful Michael Foot.'

'What exactly have you got against Foot?' asked Crossman.

'Oh nothing really,' says Waugh looking delightfully convivial over his glass of wine, 'Only that he's a grotesque exhibitionist ape whom one gets bloody tired of listening to.'

200

Ingrams gives an unexpected whinny of laughter. Waugh seems to be one of the few people capable of amusing him. Waugh on his side believes Ingrams to be the greatest master of parody since Max Beerbohm.

'What do you feel about your father's diaries?' asks Crossman. 'Personally I find them gratuitously boring. After all, there weally were some vewy intewesting conversations held in Oxford at that time, but your father seems to have omitted them entirely.'

'Masturbated, sodomised, had a very interesting conversation about Nigeria and was sick,' says Waugh urbanely.

'Well, we all enjoyed his books,' rejoined the Austrian suddenly. Hitherto he has been very quiet but now he has the air of a man who feels he ought to take umbrage but is not sure what about.

'Masturbated, sodomised, wrote a very good book and was sick,' suggested Ingrams.

'You're not one of the asterisks are you?' asked Dempster.

'Alas no,' replies the Austrian, perhaps misunderstanding the nuance of the question.

Dempster tells the story of how he'd telephoned the senile Alex Waugh in Tangier to find out if he was an asterisk. 'Have I still got my room at Whites?' was all he would bellow by way of reply.

By this time every one at the end of the table has frankly abandoned the pretence of talking amongst themselves. Coffee arrives, chairs are pushed back and cigarettes lighted. There is a definite air of waiting. Will Crossman's acrobatic logorrhoea reveal anything scandalous?

'Oh well,' says Crossman polishing off his wine with satisfaction and heading for the door. 'I'm off to the 10 minute hanging debate.'

The *Eye* watch him escape and then disperse to their hideyhole.

'Boring old Crossbum,' says Waugh as we step into the street. 'We didn't get much out of him, did we, Thomkinson?'

'Oh I don't know,' says Thomkinson thoughtfully, 'there was that rather nice corruption story he mentioned over drinks . . .'

(May 4, 1973)

201